Jews in American History

A TEACHER'S GUIDE

ABOUT THE AUTHOR

Jerome Ruderman is head of the history department at Simon Gratz High School in Philadelphia. He has a Master's degree in history and has taught American history and social studies in Philadelphia high schools since 1957. He has served as lead teacher in Philadelphia's Affective Education Program, has written social studies curriculum for the School District of Philadelphia, and since 1968 has taught American Jewish history at Adath Jeshurun Hebrew High School in Elkins Park, Pa. Mr. Ruderman is an educational consultant for Gratz College in Philadelphia and is presently on the advisory board of *Scholastic Search* magazine.

Jews in American History

A TEACHER'S GUIDE

by JEROME RUDERMAN

Published by the Anti-Defamation League of B'nai B'rith
in celebration of the Bicentennial Observance
of the United States of America

KTAV Publishing House, Inc.
New York, N. Y. 10002
and
The Anti-Defamation League of B'nai B'rith
New York, N. Y. 10016

DEDICATION

In the name of Abraham and Sarah Rabinowitz, so that others may share with them the inspiration and understanding derived from the study of Jewish History.

Library of Congress Cataloging in Publication Data

Ruderman, Jerome.
Jews in American history.

Includes bibliographies.
1. Jews in the United States—History. 2. Jews in the United States—History—Study and teaching Secondary. I. Title.
E184.J5R82 917.3'06'924 74-17500
ISBN 0-88464-007-8

Anti-Defamation League of B'nai B'rith,
315 Lexington Avenue, New York, N. Y. 10016
Printed in the United States of America

TABLE OF CONTENTS

Dedicated to

Lisette and Shelley

ACKNOWLEDGMENTS

I wish to thank Oscar Cohen, National Program Director of the Anti-Defamation League of B'nai B'rith and Stan Wexler, Director of the publications department of the ADL, for their encouragement and support. I am especially grateful to Martin Baron for his friendship, his encouragement, his invaluable suggestions and his tireless and expert editorial help. Without him this book would not have been possible. I also wish to thank Gertrude Bergman, William T. Brown, Jr., David Harrison, and Ann P. Bourman for their help.

* * *

The Anti-Defamation League of B'nai B'rith also wishes to express its appreciation to Ann P. Bourman of the Los Angeles city school system for her editorial advice and assistance.

Photo Credits

American Jewish Historical Society, 22, 25, 32, 40, 46, 56, 68, 74, 79, 94, 98, 100, 108, 112, 113, 117, 130, 136, 145, 171, 179; Congregation Beth Sholom, Elkins Park, Pa., 203; Abraham H. Foxman, 183; Hebrew Union College—Jewish Institute of Religion, 84; Jewish Theological Seminary of America, 200; Library of Congress, 112; Massachusetts Historical Society, 32; Museum of the City of New York, 136, 139; Levi Strauss and Company, 102; University of Chicago, 171; YIVO, 133, 164; Zionist Archives ,183.

INTRODUCTION

Deficiencies of History Textbooks

This book has been written to encourage the inclusion of American Jewish history in the social studies and American history curriculum of the nation's secondary schools. There is good reason for its appearance at the present time. As recently as 1970, Michael B. Kane reported that, though some improvement could be noted in the preceding decade, American history textbooks were still substantially deficient in their treatment of American Jewish history. The deficiencies include: omission, indiscriminate identification of Jews, the mere listing of Jewish contributions, the perpetuation of stereotypes which portray the Jews as a homogeneous people and as a people inordinately subject to persecution and suffering.[1]

The most obvious shortcoming is that of omission. Jews are either ignored or so casually mentioned that their role in American history and in contemporary American life is barely visible. Some recent secondary school texts have made token efforts at improvement, limited, usually, to no more than a few paragraphs. Some fail to do even that. A 1971 high school American history text, published by one of the nation's leading publishers and authored by a team of recognized scholars, made reference to Jews in only four sentences in a book of more than 800 pages. In an attempt to redress the imbalance, other texts indiscriminately identify Jews as such, even though it may be irrelevant to an understanding of the man, his career, or his role in American

1. Michael B. Kane, *Minorities in Textbooks, A Study of Their Treatment in Social Studies Texts* (Chicago, Quadrangle Books, 1970). Mr. Kane's study covered developments subsequent to the publication of Lloyd Marcus, *The Treatment of Minorities in Secondary School Textbooks* (New York, Anti-Defamation League of B'nai B'rith, 1961).

history. Ethnic identification of an individual is desirable only when it is pertinent to the point under discussion. Nor can the omission of minorities from textbooks be made right by assembling a list of minority contributions to American life. This implies that only the relatively few men and women who have won a name for themselves are worth taking notice of.

Again, Jews have, indeed, been the targets of prejudice, but they object to being portrayed merely as victims and hence as objects of pity. Exaggeration of Jewish suffering, even when it derives from the most humane intentions of writers and teachers, may give the impression that this is the normal role of the Jew in society and encourage it as natural and unavoidable.

Jews are not a race nor are they less diverse than other groups of Americans. They vary widely in their occupations, economic status, and geographic location. In 1949, the American Council on Education urged that this cardinal fact should be emphasized again and again. Yet, Michael Kane reported in 1970, twenty years later, that it is still not emphasized.

Teaching Minority History

This book has been written in the conviction that it is possible to correct the deficiencies of current textbooks while avoiding the very real pitfalls of minority history. With the decline of the melting pot approach to American history the tendency to minimize cultural differences and to dilute the role of minority groups has also waned. The new emphasis is on ethnic studies in a culturally pluralistic America with adequate treatment of the role of all minority groups. This poses two problems for social studies teachers. On one hand, they may be at a loss for appropriate ethnic materials, and on the other hand, they may be justifiably frightened by the spectre of each minority group in America demanding equal time for its own history which might be filled with persons and events of limited importance in the larger scheme of things. Given the limitations of the social studies curriculum, this procedure, if consistently followed, would reduce American history to a narrative of the problems and achievements of minority groups. The result would be unfortunate and is clearly not recommended.

There is an alternative, however. Topics in minority history should be included in the curriculum when they illuminate developments and trends in American history, generally. Inevitably, this means that those elements in the history of any minority which cannot meet this test should be excluded. If this criterion were adopted, the treatment of minorities would cease to be an act of piety or a mere listing of contributions. Minority history would take its rightful place as one element capable of illuminating major trends, concepts, and processes in the social studies. Thus, the topics chosen for inclusion in this resource guide were selected because they illuminate or underscore more general aspects of American history and to provide analogous material from the Jewish experience which might be helpful in presenting the broader scene. In so doing, it is hoped that a more accurate picture of the Jews in American history will emerge, and that the deficiencies and stereotypes cited in the Kane report will also be overcome.

Themes in American Jewish History

In the Colonial and early national period, a number of themes suggest themselves. Before there were very many Jews in America, there was already a Hebrew presence in the form of the Hebrew Bible.[2] The Judaic tradition is ignored in many American history texts, yet that tradition was one of the formative influences in Colonial New England. It helped shape early legal codes in Massachusetts, as well as the close alliance of church and state which characterized the government of the Bay Colony. The Puritans believed they had a covenant with God, as had the Israelites of the Hebrew Bible. The exodus from Egypt in search of the Promised Land was

2. Old Testament. Many Jews prefer the designation "Hebrew Bible."

taken as the prototype of that later exodus which brought the Pilgrims to the New World. The Biblical emphasis on the supremacy of the Divine Law, was a valuable tool in the hands of people who were in revolt against the Crown of England.

The first Jews to establish a community in the Colonies arrived in New Amsterdam in 1654, twenty-three refugees from the Spanish Inquisition, who arrived here via Brazil. Their arrival in America, together with that of other minorities, is important in developing the theme of immigration as a factor in American history. In very few other nations in modern times has the immigrant been as important as he has in America, where he typically came either seeking a haven from persecution or in search of economic opportunity or both. Also, the presence of the Jew in America at this early date helps illuminate the topic of cultural pluralism, the simultaneous coexistence in America of disparate racial, religious, and ethnic groups, in contrast to the far more homogeneous populations of other nations, whose assimilation into the mainstream, successful or unsuccessful, as the case may be, has proved one of the central problems in our national life. The Jewish experience clearly illustrates the theme of racial, religious, and ethnic diversity which has been a feature of American life from the outset.

The reception which the earliest Jews received in America was mixed and suggests a theme which continued well into the nineteenth century—that America was not always a land of religious liberty and equality. Separation of church and state had to be achieved; it was not always there. Jews were welcomed in liberal colonies, such as Rhode Island, Pennsylvania, Georgia, and South Carolina, which were not founded on exclusive adherence to one church, but they were excluded from those colonies that were. Puritan Massachusetts, for example, had no meaningful Jewish community before the Revolutionary War. New Amsterdam reflects a compromise between these two poles, as Jews were compelled to struggle against local intolerance for almost every right granted them.

The achievement of freedom of conscience, the separation

of church and state, and the abolition of religious tests as qualification for holding public office was not a struggle of the Jews, alone, but rather the struggle of religious minorities, among whom were Jews, Quakers, Catholics, Lutherans, and others. The first Amendment to the Constitution which protects religious liberty and prohibits an establishment of religion had as one of its roots the religious conflicts and persecution of dissidents which at times characterized Colonial life. Only one Jew was ever elected to any Continental assembly or congress. The Jewish experience in early America, with its dual quality of acceptance and exclusion, as was true of other minorities, helps to illustrate this theme.

The significance of the Jew in the transition from Colonial to Republican America, however, extends beyond the achievement of religious liberty, important as that was; it encompasses the basic meaning of the Revolution for all the colonists. Prior to the Revolution the colonists were subjects, governed ultimately by a king in whose making they played no part. In the Revolution, democratic, secular authority replaced the authority of the monarchy which had rested in part on the consent of the established church. The former colonists had become citizens who elected their governors, and because they voted as citizens, and not as members of a religious community, there was no longer any reason for excluding religious minorities from civic life. Thus, if we once understand why the Jews and other religious minorities were enfranchised by the Revolution, we have understood why the colonists, generally, were, as well.

During the era of the Revolutionary War, though numerically few, Jews were becoming visible. They participated in, fought in, and died in the same battles and campaigns as did other Americans. There were Jewish Patriots and there were Jewish Loyalists. There was, even at this early date, no such thing as a typical American Jew. Some were ridden out of town by angry mobs, others were lauded for heroism in the Continental Army.

The next major topic that might be fruitfully incorporated

into general accounts of American history, is the German Jewish migration of the mid-nineteenth century, which lends itself to a continuation of the themes of immigration and pluralism and also suggests the theme of America as a land of opportunity. In 1840, there were perhaps 15,000 Jews in America, mainly of Spanish and Portuguese origin. By 1880, the number had risen to 250,000, swelled by substantial numbers of Jewish immigrants from Germany. Though their numbers were still small, their history illuminates the larger scene—immigration, the western frontier, and American economic development. These immigrants were, for the most part, quite poor and many of them fanned out across the continent seeking economic opportunity. Jews were present in the California gold fields; they fought in the Mexican War; they were buffalo-hunters, ranchers, miners, photographers, newspaper editors; they participated in every aspect of frontier life. Substantial numbers became peddlers and their achievement sheds light on the nature of American capitalism. After accumulating a bare minimum of capital, many became shopkeepers and a few managed to found what have since become some of the largest department stores in America.

The Jewish community epitomized the zeal with which groups in America have founded private, voluntary organizations, and the German-Jewish immigrants largely inaugurated this development within the American Jewish community. Many of the congregations, schools, hospitals, free loan societies, and defense organizations were founded by German-Jewish immigrants or their immediate descendants. In some ways these institutions have served as models for other ethnic groups.

During the Civil War, Jews were, as during the Revolution, a diverse people, reflecting regional attitudes rather than a common Jewish outlook. Northern Jews tended to oppose slavery while Southern Jews tended to support it. Their response to the war is an excellent example of the sectionalism which prevailed during the pre-war years. As was true generally, Jews could not agree whether the Bible condemned or condoned slavery.

The anti-Semitism which surfaced during the war years and immediately thereafter, sheds light on the nature of scapegoating, particularly during periods of national crisis. Even though American history has not been free of anti-Semitism, there is an important difference in this respect between Europe and America. In the United States anti-Semitism has been almost consistently repudiated by the government, as contrasted to the classical government-sponsored anti-Semitism of Europe where bloody attacks on Jews began in medieval times and culminated in the Holocaust, conceived and perpetrated by the Third Reich. Nonetheless, American anti-Semitism has led to serious discrimination in housing, education, employment, and acceptance in certain social groups.

The Jewish population in America between 1880 and 1920 grew from 250,000 to 3,500,000. The increase is accounted for largely by the immigration to America of 2,000,000 Jewish refugees from Russia and other parts of East Central Europe. The eastern European Jews, unlike the German Jews before them, did not begin as peddlers. The majority sought employment in shops and factories, and generally settled in New York and a few other large cities, where they entered the needle trades in substantial numbers. The Jewish experience at this point illustrates several important developments in modern American history: the acculturation of immigrant groups, urbanization, and the development of the trade union movement, all of which illustrate the interaction between the resources an immigrant brings with him and the requirements and opportunities of his new environment. Many Jews entered the clothing industry because they had worked in the garment industry in Russia, because the industry was rapidly expanding in America, and because the owners were often German Jews. They created trade unions not only because conditions in industrial

America made them necessary, but also because some Jews had been active trade unionists and socialists before immigrating to America.

American Judaism evolved steadily during the nineteenth and early twentieth centuries. While the religiosity of many Jews has waned in comparison to that of previous generations, the striking feature of the Jewish community has remained its determination to preserve Jewish identity, which raises the problem of assimilation in a pluralistic society. Like other minority groups, Jews have been faced with a conflict generated by the desire to be as much like their neighbors as possible, while maintaining a separate identity as American Jews.

The Jewish experience in America is thus intricately woven into the fabric of general American history. This book concentrates on those aspects of Jewish history which offer material with which to illuminate many important general themes and concepts. It is not proposed that these are the only opportunities suggested by American Jewish historical material, nor for one moment is it suggested that these concepts and themes are to be illustrated by the Jewish experience exclusively. On the contrary, it is because Jews have shared these experiences with many other groups and with the larger society that they have a valid place in the textbooks and classrooms of America's schools.

Bibliography and Audio-Visual Materials

The basic reference bibliography which follows this introduction and the more specific bibliographies which follow each chapter include only a few of the many books about Jews and Jewish history, not necessarily those referred to in writing this book. Selections were made according to the criteria of suitability, availability, and balance. Care was taken to select the most pertinent materials and those which are generally available in large municipal or university libraries or are of recent enough publication to be available in bookstores. Consequently many relatively obscure titles have not been listed. An effort has been made to maintain topical balance which may also account for the omission of some worthwhile books. Others may have been left out through simple human error. All listings are annotated and indicate the major thrust or relevance of a book as well as its suitability. Those recommended for junior high school students will generally be suitable for older students with reading difficulties. Though this book is primarily intended for teachers it is also suitable for adults, generally. The word "teacher" in the bibliographical evaluations should therefore be taken to refer to adults, as well.

In the selection of audio-visual materials the same criteria of suitability, availability, and balance were employed, although availability will depend on the distributor who is identified in each listing. In most cases films are for sale or rental and filmstrips for sale, only. Teachers should inquire about price and availability well in advance of their needs. All films are 16 mm; all filmstrips are 35 mm. Many of the audio-visual materials listed have been produced by Jewish sources and were originally intended for Jewish audiences. This fact should present no problem for non-Jewish or mixed religious groups. In fact the teacher might include "purpose" as part of his introduction of such materials and utilize this fact to good advantage in analyzing the production.

DISCUSSION QUESTIONS AND STUDENT ACTIVITIES

1. Conduct a discussion on the purpose of ethnic studies. For example: to develop ethnic pride, to fill in omissions, to "tell it like it is," to correct distortions and stereotypes, etc. See *Minorities in Textbooks,* by Michael B. Kane (listed in Basic Bibliography). Have students list, in order of importance, reasons for studying various ethnic groups. Discuss why they may differ from one group to another.
2. Have students analyze their American history textbooks (and others, if available), and compile a report on how frequently Jews are mentioned, in what connection, and if such reference is pertinent to understanding their role

in American history. Refer to *Minorities in Textbooks,* by Michael B. Kane (listed in Basic Bibliography). Conduct a discussion about why Jews are generally omitted from the students' books. (This will be true in nearly all cases.) Have students write letters to publishers calling attention to such deficiencies.

3. Discuss and formulate a definition of who is a Jew and what is Judaism. This might lend itself to small group work.
4. Ask each student in the class to guess how many Jews live in the United States and when the first Jews arrived. Inform them that there are approximately six million Jews in America today and that Jews first arrived in New Amsterdam in 1654. How accurate were their guesses? What preconceptions help explain their errors? Encourage discussion.
5. Have a committee of students prepare an itinerary for a class trip to Jewish points of interest in or near your city. A good source will be *A Jewish Tourist's Guide to the U.S.* by Bernard Postal and Lionel Koppman (See Basic Bibliography). The committee should learn as much as possible about each place to be visited and brief the class before the trip.

BASIC BIBLIOGRAPHY

American Jewish Yearbook (Jewish Publication Society, Philadelphia, 1899-present). Published annually. This is a useful reference work containing a review of the year's events in American and world Jewish life, trends, directory and statistical information, special articles, biographies, and bibliographies. Many early issues are still pertinent for reference. Volume 40 contains a subject index to special articles in preceding volumes. Beginning with volume 44 each volume contains an American Jewish Bibliography. Recommended as a research tool for teachers and capable high school students.

Blau, Joseph L. and Baron, Salo, (Eds.), *The Jews of the United States: 1790-1840; A Documentary History* (Columbia University Press, New York, 1963). An excellent collection of source documents arranged topically with an introductory preface to each. Includes many topics dealt with in this guide. Suitable for original research projects. Recommended for teachers and capable high school students.

Dimont, Max I., *Jews, God and History* (Simon and Schuster, New York, 1962; also in paperback, Signet Books, New York, 1962). A dramatic, highly readable general history of the Jews. Ideal for background. Chapter 27 is an excellent quick summary of American Jewish history. For teachers and high school students.

Eisenberg, Azriel, *The Golden Land* (Thomas Yoseloff, New York, 1964). An anthology of fiction, essays, and verse giving a literary portrait of Jewish life in America from 1654 to the present. Includes 85 selections by dozens of authors. Eisenberg uses a diversified approach and does not limit his material only to prominent Jews. For teachers and better than average high school students.

Friedman, Lee M., *Jewish Pioneers and Patriots* (Jewish Publication Society, Philadelphia, 1955). A well-written book about an unusual selection of Jewish pioneers and patriots. Provides fresh insights into American Jewish history. Recommended for capable high school students and teachers.

Friedman, Lee M., *Pilgrims in a New Land* (Jewish Publication Society, Philadelphia, 1948). A highly readable, yet academically sound work. Covers a number of important topics in American history relative to the Jews and includes much useful biographical material. The book is enhanced by an abundant use of original documents. Recommended for teachers and high school students.

Gay, Ruth, *Jews in America, A Short History* (Basic Books, New York, 1965). A "mini-history" of Jewish America written in a pleasant, easy style, suitable for junior and senior high school students. Chapters 1 through 4 provide a skimpy coverage of early American Jewish history. The remainder of the book deals with anti-Semitism and the Nazi era, concluding with a sociological look at the contemporary Jewish community in America.

Glazer, Nathan, *American Judaism* (University of Chicago Press, Chicago, Second Edition, 1972, also in paperback). This is a penetrating historical survey of Judaism in America dealing with broad sociological questions of Jewish identity and the Jewish religion. The book is heavily weighted toward the contemporary scene, describing the characteristics and values of second-generation Jewish immigrants and their rise in American society. Recommended for teachers and capable high school students.

Grayzel, Solomon, *A History of the Jews* (Jewish Publication Society of America, Philadelphia, Second Edition, 1968, also in paperback). A comprehensive general history of the Jewish people from the sixth century B.C.E.[3] to the birth of the modern state of Israel in 1948. Several chapters deal specifically with American Jewish history; others discuss the European background for Jewish migration to the United States. Written by a Jew for Jews, but recommended for teachers and high school students of all faiths.

Handlin, Oscar, *Adventure in Freedom: Three Hundred Years of Jewish Life in America* (McGraw-Hill, New York, 1954). Professor Handlin, a Pulitzer prize winner, provides a well-balanced, professional historian's approach to his subject. The book is particularly good on the East European Jewish immigration after 1881. Highly recommended for teachers and capable high school students.

Handlin, Oscar, *American Jews: Their Story* (Anti-Defamation League of B'nai B'rith, New York, (paperback). A very brief history of the Jews in America. For junior and senior high school students.

3. B.C.E., Before the Common Era, is equivalent to B.C. C.E., the Common Era, is equivalent to A.D. Many Jews prefer these to the Christian designations.

Kane, Michael P., *Minorities in Textbooks: A Study of Their Treatment in Social Studies Texts* (Quadrangle, Chicago, 1970, paperback). A study of secondary school textbooks sponsored by the Anti-Defamation League of B'nai B'rith. Mr. Kane documents the neglect and distortion of minority history in the United States. Chapter I deals with the Jewish minority; section E., "Jewish Life in America," is most pertinent. This book is basic reading for any teacher contemplating the inclusion of ethnic materials in American history courses. Suitable for junior and senior high students, as well.

Karp, Deborah, *Heros of American Jewish History* (Ktav Publishing House, Inc. and Anti-Defamation League of B'nai B'rith, New York, 1973). The achievements of notable American Jews, in their historical setting. Illustrated. For junior and senior high school students.

Karp, Abraham J., *The Jewish Experience in America: Selected Studies from the Publications of the American Jewish Historical Society* (Ktav Publishing House, New York, 1969). This is a five-volume set containing selected articles from 57 volumes of the publications of the American Jewish Historical Society. Volume I is entitled "The Colonial Period," Volume II, "In the Early Republic," Volume III, "The Emerging Community," Volume IV, "The Era of Immigration," and Volume V, "At Home In America." Written by professional historians, this set contains a gold mine of information for teachers and superior students who may wish to delve further into specific topics.

Learsi, Rufus, *The Jews in America: A History* (Ktav, New York, 1972. Originally published in 1954, this is one of the best books available on American Jewish history. It is thorough, accurate, and well-written. It tends, however, to stress organizational features of American Judaism, overemphasizes European matters, and is inordinately concerned with Zionism. It contains very little contemporary sociological or demographic material. Nonetheless, highly recommended for teachers and capable high school students.

Levinger, Lee J., *A History of the Jews in the United States* (Union of American Hebrew Congregations, New York, 1961). A basic text for junior and senior high school students in Jewish schools. Suitable for non-Jews, as well. Originally published in 1930 and revised in 1961, many of the books cited in the chapter-by-chapter bibliography are out of print and difficult or impossible to find. Review questions at the end of each chapter may be of some use. The book leaves much to be desired stylistically, but is, nonetheless, very informative. Teachers will find it a handy reference book.

Marcus, Jacob R., *Studies in American Jewish History* (Hebrew Union College Press, Cincinnati, 1969). A collection of essays by an outstanding American-Jewish historian. Chapters 1, 2 and 4 are particularly useful for general historiographical discussion. Specific topics covered are: Periodization of American Jewish History, and Themes and Trends in American Jewish History. Recommended for teachers and better than average students.

Pessin, Deborah, *History of the Jews in America* (United Synagogue of America, New York, 1957). A text for use in Jewish schools, but appropriate for all faiths. Well-written at the junior high reading level. Questions, activities, and bibliography following each chapter will be helpful to teachers.

Postal, Bernard and Koppman, Lionel, *A Jewish Tourist's Guide to the U.S.* (Jewish Publication Society, Philadelphia, 1954). A combination history and guidebook in one volume. The authors provide a popular and complete historical survey for each state (48) and the District of Columbia, together with pertinent points of interest in each. The book contains much historical and biographical material about Jews in American history. Though somewhat dated, it should be helpful to teachers in planning trips and visits and in identifying places to which students may write for specific information. Highly recommended for teachers and high school students. (A new edition is planned for 1976.)

Sachar, Howard Morley, *The Course of Modern Jewish History* (World Publishing Company, Cleveland, 1958; also a Delta paperback). Jewish history in Europe and America from the 18th century to the present. Both scholarly and readable. For teachers and capable high school students.

Schappes, Morris U. (ed.), *A Documentary History of the Jews in the United States, 1654-1875* (Citadel Press, New York, 1950). A valuable collection of source documents. Each is preceded by the editor's introduction. Recommended for teachers and superior high school students.

Schappes, Morris U., *The Jews in the United States, A Pictorial History, 1654 to the Present* (Citadel Press, New York, 1958). A profusely illustrated history. The material is interestingly arranged and suitable for high school students as well as teachers. Excellent for research projects.

Seldin, Ruth, *Teacher's Guide to Jews and Their Religion* (Ktav Publishing House, New York, 1970). A resource guide prepared for Catholic high schools by the Anti-Defamation League of B'nai B'rith. Suitable for Jews and Protestants, as well. Part I consists of transcripts of six filmed lectures about Jews and Judaism which are available from the ADL (315 Lexington Ave., New York, N. Y. 10016 or from regional ADL offices). Each is by a reputable Jewish authority. Part II is a helpful teacher's guide by Ruth Seldin which provides ample suggestions for classroom activities and discussion topics. Includes a useful bibliography of books and audio-visual materials. Though it is primarily for teachers, high school students will profit from it, as well.

Sklare, Marshall, Ed., *The Jews: Social Patterns of an American Group* (The Free Press, New York, 1958). A scholarly anthology which treats numerous sociological aspects of the American Jewish community. It deals with the Jewish historical setting, Jewish demography, the Jewish community, the Jewish religion, and psychological and cultural aspects of American Jewish life. This is a basic sociological reference work for teachers and only the most capable high school students doing research. Not recommended for the casual reader.

St. John, Robert, *Jews, Justice and Judaism* (Doubleday, New York, 1969). A very readable narrative history of the role Jews played in shaping America. Popularly written, yet full of useful information. The principal emphasis is the Jewish contribution to social justice in the United States. Highly recommended for teachers and high school students.

Suhl, Yuri, *An Album of the Jews in America* (Franklin Watts and the Anti-Defamation League of B'nai B'rith, New York, 1972, paperback). An illustrated history of the Jews in America from the earliest times to the present. The illustrations include numerous historical photographs. Suitable for elementary and junior high school students.

BASIC AUDIO-VISUAL MATERIALS

The American Jew: A Tribute to Freedom. An edited kinescope film based on an original one-hour program produced by CBS-TV, 1958, 45 minutes, black and white, narrated by Jeff Chandler, sponsored and distributed by the Anti-Defamation League of B'nai B'rith, 315 Lexington Avenue, New York, N. Y. 10016 (also ADL regional offices). This film tells the story of the Jew in the United States by means of the contributions of outstanding American Jewish personalities. For high school audiences.

The Jewish Audio-Visual Review, Eighteenth Annual Edition, 1973. (The National Council on Jewish Audio-Visual Materials of the American Association for Jewish Education, 114 Fifth Avenue, New York, N. Y. 10003.) This is a comprehensive listing of Jewish audio-visual materials with descriptions, evaluations, specific recommendations, and pertinent information about source, price and/or rental charge. Many free or inexpensive items are listed. Not confined to American Jewish history. The only such work available. Highly recommended for teachers.

The Jews, a filmstrip produced and distributed by Warren Schloat Productions, Inc., Pleasantville, New York, 10570, 1965. Part 3 of the set *Minorities Have Made America Great,* produced under the name WASP Filmstrips, 61 frames, color, with accompanying LP record narrated by Jim Ameche. This filmstrip traces the three major periods of Jewish migration to the United States. Highlights the story of Levi Strauss, the peddler who produced Levi trousers. Though it exaggerates the role of Jewish contributors, it does provide, nonetheless, a good overview of American Jewish history. Highly recommended for junior and senior high school audiences.

Jews in America. Produced and distributed by the Anti-Defamation League of B'nai B'rith, 315 Lexington Ave., New York, N. Y. 10016, 1973. Part I, (20 minutes, 100 frames, color) "The Golden Door," begins with the earliest Jewish settlers in America and extends to approximately the 1880's. Part II, (22 minutes, 101 frames) "Inside the Golden Door," continues the story to the present. This set of filmstrips is technically outstanding. The soundtrack is superb, featuring flawless narration and expert integration of music. The choice of photographs, documents and illustrations is excellent. Though it mentions numerous Jewish personalities, it successfully integrates American Jewish history into general American history, documenting the fact that Jews were there. A dramatic presentation, almost like a motion picture. Highly recommended for junior and senior high school students.

Rendevous With Freedom. A documentary film produced by ABC-TV, 1973. 37 minutes, color. Available from the Anti-Defamation League of B'nai B'rith, 315 Lexington Avenue, New York, N. Y. 10016. Commentary by ABC news correspondent Herbert Kaplow. Narration, readings and songs by Zero Mostel, Sam Jaffe, Marian Seldes, and George Segal. This excellent film tells the story of Jewish immigration to the New World from 1654 to the present. Sequences filmed in Europe explain the persecution, fear and economic pressures that forced Jews to emigrate. Traces the development of American Jewry, its contributions to and participation in the major events of the nation's history. Depicts the cultural and spiritual legacies left to all Americans by Jewish immigrants. Vivid period paintings, engravings, and photographs enhance this excellent film. Recommended for junior and senior high school audiences.

Three Hundred Years: Memorable Events in American Jewish History, a filmstrip produced by Victor Kayfetz Productions, Inc., 1954. 45 frames, color, includes 2 copies of teacher's guide, accompanying 12-inch LP recorded narration also available. Distributed by the Commission on Jewish Education, Union of American Hebrew Congregations, 838 Fifth Avenue, New York, N. Y. 10021. The highlights of American Jewish history, including the Colonial experience, the westward movement, and the development of the American Jewish community and its religious institutions. Tends to emphasize the biographical method but maintains interest throughout. The script is lengthy, but the production is suitable for junior high and high school audiences.

Who Are The American Jews? A film produced (in cooperation with the Archdiocese of New York) and distributed by the Anti-Defamation League of B'nai B'rith, 315 Lexington Avenue, New York, N. Y. 10016, 1969. 30 minutes, black and white. Dore Schary, playwright, producer, director, presents a profile of the American Jewish community and its growth and development over 300 years. In his lecture, illustrated with archive prints and rare photographs, Mr. Schary surveys the diversity within the American Jewish community which is reflected by its involvement in every level of American life. He analyzes its involvement with philanthropic and human relations concerns and assesses its relationship to the State of Israel. Recommended for junior and senior high school students.

PRELUDE

Jews constitute a religious, cultural and ethnic group that originated in the land that is today Israel. In 70 C.E.[1] the Jewish state in Palestine was destroyed as a political unit by the Romans. Though some Jews remained in the area, most dispersed throughout the world, many to Babylonia, later to Spain, and eventually to all the nations of western and eastern Europe.

Jews in the Diaspora (lands outside Palestine) hoped some day to return to their original homeland. The founding of the state of Israel has made this possible for many. For the six million Jews who live in America, this nation has been so hospitable that few seriously consider leaving to live in Israel. A brief glance at the history of the Jews in Europe may usefully serve as a prologue to the story of the Jews in America.

For centuries Jews in Europe were persecuted. During the Middle Ages they were scorned and segregated, even attacked and killed, because they refused to accept Christianity. In modern times they have often been scapegoats for society's ills. They have frequently been confined to ghettos, consistently barred from owning land, forbidden to work in many crafts and professions, excluded from universities and government, scorned in social life, subject to periodic slaughter, and at times expelled as a group. No wonder, then, that from the earliest days of settlement in the New World, Jews came in search of a home free from tyranny and persecution.

The specific train of events that brought the first Jews to America stretches back to the early eighth century when Moslems crossed the Straits of Gibraltar, conquered Spain, and ushered in a new era of peaceful relations with the Jews, who by the ninth century had shifted the center of their

1. C.E., the Common Era. Equivalent to A.D. See note above, p. 12.

community from Babylonia to Spain. By the thirteenth century Jewish life there had begun to decline as the Moslems were slowly driven out and an era of Christian fanaticism set in.

By the early thirteenth century the Iberian peninsula, with the exception of Moorish Granada in the south, was entirely in Christian hands. Jews continued to flourish in what was still the most favorable climate for them in Europe. But in the fourteenth century, increasing competition developed between Christian and Jewish merchants in the cities. Christians, envious of the wealth many Jews had acquired, and resentful of their role as advisers, tax collectors, and financiers to the king, insisted on local laws restricting the religious liberty of Jews. Anti-Jewish violence, common elsewhere in Europe, began to erupt in Spain. Jews were blamed for the Black Plague. Massacres followed and Jews were accused of ritual murder to obtain Christian blood for the Passover feast. In 1391, mobs inflamed by a fanatic archdeacon sacked the Jewish section of Seville. Violence, bloodletting and destruction followed as the archdeacon led mobs from city to city, invading Jewish neighborhoods and synagogues and offering the Jews death or baptism. The Jewish communities of Seville, Cordova, Toledo, and others were almost wiped out as the attacks spread throughout the country. In 1391 alone, two hundred thousand "New Christians" were baptized. For many it was only a meaningless ritual. They practiced Christianity in public and Judaism in private. Christians, doubting their sincerity, labelled them *Marrano,* meaning "pig." In the fifteenth century, new outbreaks of violence produced new converts, many of whom rose rapidly in politics, in the military, in university life, and in the Church itself. *Marranos* generally handled the financial administration of the kingdom and were often close to the seats of power. Many married into the best families of Spain. But they were suspected of practicing Judaism in secret and of maintaining links with the remaining Jewish community. In many cases this was true. To terminate this, the Spanish Inquisition was established in 1478. Torture was used to extract confessions, and public burnings of convicted heretics were commonplace. The Church said that each day a heretic lived in "sin" only added to his ultimate punishment in hell. Thus, the executions were intended to lessen his sufferings. It was also a means for the Church to vastly expand its riches, as the property of convicted heretics was confiscated.

For the Spanish authorities, another danger was the Jewish community itself, which, they feared, was secretly encouraging the loyalty of the *Marranos* to Judaism. Yet the monarchs hesitated to order their expulsion, for Jews were still important in the government, and their support was needed in the campaign against the Moors in Granada. However, when that last bit of Moslem territory fell in 1492, the expulsion was ordered. The last boatload of exiles left on the same tide and from the same harbor as Columbus; ironically, a door to a new world was being opened just as the door to the old one was slamming shut.

Most of the fleeing Spanish Jews sought refuge in Portugal, where thousands more were forced into baptism, creating another *Marrano* class. But in 1497 they were expelled from Portugal. Others went to the Turkish Empire, which included Palestine, where they were warmly welcomed. Still others fled to Morocco and Egypt, Italy or Holland. A few, as we shall see, made their way to America. By 1500 there were no professing Jews in Spain or Portugal. The Inquisition continued to hunt *Marranos* until the nineteenth century, but their loyalty to Judaism endured. As late as World War I, communities of *Marranos* were discovered in remote parts of northern Portugal and Spain, still practicing a secret religion recognizable as Judaism.

Thousands of Jews perished at the hands of the Inquisition. Countless others were forced or frightened into the Church. The greatest Jewish community in Europe, numbering perhaps a quarter of a million people, was completely destroyed. Some of the Spanish Jews who survived built a community in America.

דקדוק

לשון עברית

DICKDOOK LESHON GNEBREET.

A

GRAMMAR

OF THE

Hebrew Tongue,

BEING

An ESSAY

To bring the Hebrew Grammar into English,

to Facilitate the

INSTRUCTION

Of all thoſe who are deſirous of acquiring a clear Idea of this

Primitive Tongue

by their own Studies;

In order to their more diſtinct Acquaintance with the SACRED ORACLES of the Old Teſtament, according to the Original. And Publiſhed more eſpecially for the Uſe of the STUDENTS of *HARVARD-COLLEGE* at *Cambridge*, in NEW-ENGLAND.

נחבר והוגת בעיון נמרץ על ידי

יהודה מוניש

Compoſed and accurately Corrected,

By JUDAH MONIS, *M. A.*

BOSTON, N. England

Printed by JONAS GREEN, and are to be Sold by the AUTHOR at his Houſe in *Cambridge*. MDCCXXXV.

Title page of Hebrew *Grammar* of Judah Monis at Harvard, 1735.

CHAPTER I

THE COLONIAL WORLD

*

IMPORTANT EVENTS

1654 Twenty-three Jews arrive in New Amsterdam, establishing the first Jewish settlement in North America.

1703 In South Carolina, Jews vote in a general election for the first time in the history of the Western world.

1730 The first regular synagogue in North America is completed in New Amsterdam by Congregation Shearith Israel (Remnant of Israel).

1763 America's oldest surviving Jewish house of worship, the Touro Synagogue, is dedicated at Newport, Rhode Island.

Spanish and Portuguese Colonies

With the fall of Constantinople to the Ottoman Turks in 1453, merchandise brought overland from the Far East was subject to heavy taxation and banditry as it passed through the Turkish Empire. New transportation routes sprang up, relying instead on shipment from port cities at the eastern end of the Mediterranean to port cities in Europe. Venice and Genoa, in northern Italy, were ideally situated to funnel the goods of the Orient into the heart of Europe, and they became extremely wealthy in the process. Spain and Portugal, determined to wrest this supremacy from the Italians, channeled their efforts into finding new ways to reach the Orient. In Portugal Prince Henry founded a school of navigation and Spain financed Columbus in what was to be the greatest geographic discovery of modern history. These commercial rivalries of the fifteenth century were played out against a background of terror and expulsion for thousands of Spanish Moslems and Jews. Yet, despite this, Jews were of significant help to Columbus. He received much information from Jewish voyagers and scientists. While in Portugal, he studied the charts of Judah Cresques, known as the "map Jew," who later headed Prince Henry's school of navigation. He used the astronomical tables of the celebrated Jewish astronomer, Abraham Zacuto. A number of Jews helped finance the expedition. Luis de Santangel, chancellor of the royal court, and Gabriel Sanchez, the chief treasurer of Aragon, both *Marranos,* were principal backers. Two of the most distinguished Jews in Spain, Abraham Senior and Isaac Abravanel, were among the first to support him. Luis de Torres, the official interpreter for the expedition, was a *Marrano.* De Torres's knowledge of Hebrew, Arabic and Aramaic ("Oriental" tongues) was expected to help him converse with the inhabitants of lands in "Asia." He became the first European to settle in the New World when he chose not to return with Columbus. He spent the rest of his life in Cuba. At least four other *Marranos* sailed with Columbus, two of them physicians.

Marranos, like Luis de Torres, no doubt saw in the New World a haven beyond the reach of the Inquisition, but the Inquisition followed them to the New World. Converted Jews were frequently executed in the Spanish colonies, and in Portuguese Brazil those suspected of practicing Judaism were sent to Portugal for trial. *Marranos* in Brazil lived in constant fear until the seventeenth century when the Dutch conquered the colony and offered protection and religious liberty to all who would accept their rule. *Marranos* rejoiced and openly returned to Judaism, for the Dutch were well-known for their liberalism. (So many Jews lived in Amsterdam that it had become known as "New Jerusalem.")

In 1630 the Dutch captured Recife, Brazil. Immigration increased the population to 5,000, about 1,500 of whom were Jews. Their new freedom was epitomized by the construction of a synagogue, *Zur Israel* (Rock of Israel), and by the arrival in 1642 of the first rabbi in the western hemisphere,

An astrolabe with Hebrew lettering, made by a Jewish astronomer for Alfonso, King of Castile.

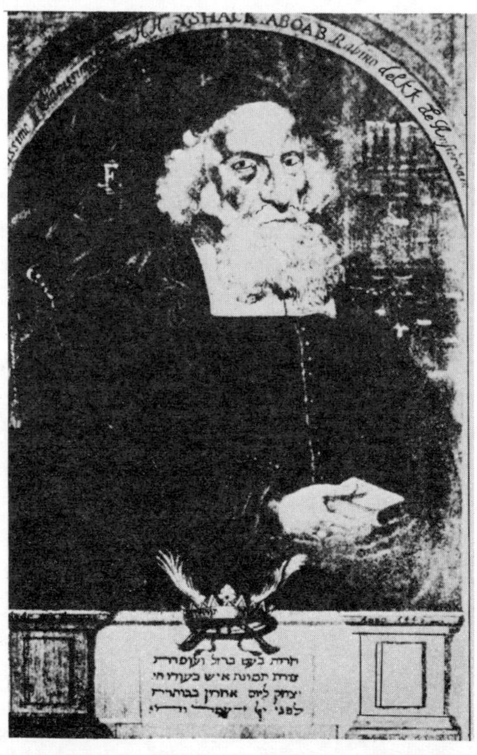

Isaac Aboab da Fonseca, rabbi in Amsterdam and the first rabbi to come to the western hemisphere.

Isaac Aboab da Fonseca, as well as a cantor and a large party of Jews from Amsterdam. Thus emerged the first Jewish community on the soil of the New World.

In 1654 the Portuguese reconquered Recife. The Jews participated in the unsuccessful defense of their homes. Their heroism was documented by Rabbi Aboab in the first Hebrew book written in the New World, *The Great Remembrance*. Echoing the great expulsion of a century and a half earlier, the Jews were given the choice of baptism or exile, and as before, the majority chose exile rather than the clandestine life of the *Marrano*. Most returned to Holland. Others fled to Dutch and English colonies in the Caribbean.

New York

In 1654, twenty-three Jews from Recife arrived in New Amsterdam. They constituted the first Jewish community on North American soil. Acceptance of Jews in the English colonies varied directly with the liberalism of the colony and inversely with its religious fervor. In the liberal colonies, such as Rhode Island, Pennsylvania, Georgia, and South Carolina, outstanding leaders like Roger Williams, William Penn, James Oglethorpe, and the British philosopher John Locke, were influential and minorities were welcomed. In others, such as Puritan Massachusetts, and Virginia, where the Church of England was entrenched, no early Jewish community developed.

New Amsterdam fell somewhere in the middle of the spectrum. There, Dutch Reformed preachers were exceedingly intolerant of all who professed religions other than their own, with the single exception of English Presbyterians whose Calvinism seemed sufficiently orthodox to them. On the other hand, the Dutch West India Company had initially founded the colony as a profit-making venture. Its officers, among them several Jews, reflected the liberalism of Holland. They instructed Peter Stuyvesant, the governor of the colony, to let variations in religion "pass in silence," which he grudgingly was obliged to do. Thus, New Netherlands followed a middle-of-the-road policy toward minorities.

Stuyvesant had wanted the Jews expelled. If he allowed them liberty and freedom, he reasoned, so must he allow the same to "Lutherans and Baptists." But the Board of Directors disagreed and the twenty-three were permitted to remain, providing they took care of their own poor. Stuyvesant insisted they live "as close together as possible" in what became known as "Jews' Alley." He denied them the most elementary property and business rights and refused permission to erect a synagogue. This policy was part of a general prohibition against public religious gatherings, other than those of the Dutch Reformed Church. It was even enforced against Dutch Lutherans in the colony. The Jews formed Congregation *Shearith Israel* (Remnant of Israel), which continues to flourish at the present day, and conducted religious services in their own homes, which Stuyvesant was under orders to tolerate.

From the outset, minority rights were hard won. Jews were not permitted to perform military service with Christians, but were required to pay a tax in lieu of service. Asser Levy, an important Jewish leader who became one of the town's wealthiest and most respected citizens, and Jacob Barsimson, who had arrived a month before the Recife group, petitioned for the right to stand guard in defense of the town. They ultimately won their case. Levy had been a full burgher in Amsterdam and on appeal won for himself and his fellow Jews the status of burghers with a limited right of civil participation in the colony, though full equality was yet to come.

In 1664 when the British captured New Amsterdam and renamed it New York, the status of the Jews did not immediately change, but discrimination was gradually relaxed. By 1682 Jews were able to use a rented house as a synagogue. At that time there were 855 families in New York and only twenty of them were Jewish. There were five churches.

It is interesting to note that in 1711 Abraham de Lucena and six other New York Jews contributed to a fund for the construction of a steeple on Trinity Episcopal Church in New York. In Philadelphia some years later a group of Christians helped pay off the mortgage on a synagogue there. Interfaith cooperation had already begun despite the small number of Jews in the colonies at that time.

In 1727 Jews achieved a further degree of civic equality in New York when the General Assembly of the colony exempted them from uttering the words, "upon the true faith of a Christian" in the oath of allegiance to the king. The following year Congregation *Shearith Israel* was finally permitted to build a synagogue which was completed and dedicated in 1730.

Rhode Island

Newport, Rhode Island, became the second largest Jewish community in America. Rhode Island's charter declared that no person should be molested because of his religion, and its outstanding liberal leader, Roger Williams, specifically invited Jews to settle there. The tolerance of the colony was unmistakable, and Jews, together with other minorities, thrived.

The Newport Jewish community dates from 1658, with the arrival of fifteen families from Holland. Others came from Portugal, Spain, and Poland. Congregational records show a number of merchants and traders. Two of the most outstanding families were Lopez from Portugal and Rivera from Spain. Both families had been *Marranos* for eight generations. Jacob Rodriguez Rivera introduced the manufacture of spermaceti candles and later invented the sperm oil lamp, creating vast new markets for the whaling industry. His son-in-law, Aaron Lopez, "the merchant prince of New England," owned a fleet of thirty transatlantic ships and more than a hundred coastal vessels at the time of his death. In 1763, the year the French and Indian War ended, Congregation *Yeshuat Israel* (Salvation of Israel) dedicated the Newport synagogue. Isaac Touro became its first cantor. His sons, Judah and Abraham, endowed the building, ensuring the preservation of what is today the oldest surviving Jewish house of worship in the United States. In 1947 the Touro synagogue was designated a national historic shrine. An active congregation still worships there.

Pennsylvania

In the eighteenth century, Philadelphia was the most cosmopolitan Colonial city in America. William Penn had founded his Quaker experiment under a charter of toleration welcoming settlers of all nations and all faiths. A few Jews were there as early as 1726. Twelve years later they were numerous enough to request a cemetery, though soon after, a twenty-shilling reward was posted for information leading to the arrest of vandals who were desecrating it. Penn's successors, considerably less liberal than Penn himself, enforced a law restricting voting and office holding to Christians. Jews, nonetheless, accustomed to far worse restrictions elsewhere, considered the Quaker colony a most receptive home. In Philadelphia, Congregation *Mikveh Israel* (Hope of Israel) was organized in the 1740's. Jews also settled in Easton, Reading, Lancaster, and other towns in Pennsylvania.

Georgia

Georgia was settled by the humanitarian, James Oglethorpe, as a haven for debtors from English jails. Its charter excluded all but Protestants. At first the trustees in London opposed the admission of Jews to the colony, but Oglethorpe defended them, and put Jews in his colony on an equal footing with other settlers. As a Christian minister in Georgia noted in his journal, "Even the Jews, of whom several families are already in the country, enjoy all privileges the same as other colonists." Unlike their counterparts in New Amsterdam, they had the right from the outset to "carry muskets like the others in military style." In 1733, forty-three Jews arrived from England. Oglethorpe granted each a plot of land in Savannah. Six months later, forty Jews of Portuguese and Spanish origin arrived. They founded a congregation in Savannah in 1734. The Jewish community included

Abraham de Lyon, who imported some choice vines which produced grapes "as big as a man's thumb," and Mordecai Sheftall, the first white child born in Savannah. Sheftall later became the Jewish founding member of the Union Society, the first interfaith charity in America which united Jews, Protestants and Catholics in a common social cause.

Carolina

A draft constitution for Carolina was written by John Locke, the British philosopher whose natural rights theories influenced the Declaration of Independence. It was so liberal that it included a specific provision to protect minorities. "No person whatsoever shall disturb, molest or persecute another for his speculative opinions or his way of worship." Referring to Jews, Locke wrote, "If we allow the Jews to have private houses and dwelling places among us, why should we not allow them to have synagogues?" While his constitution excluded atheists and required everyone over seventeen years of age to have some religious affiliation, the choice was left entirely to the individual. Though his liberality was based on the prospect of attracting converts to Christianity, and though the constitution was never finally adopted, it was indicative of a spirit of toleration unrivaled elsewhere in the Colonies. In 1703 the Jews of South Carolina voted in a general election for the first time in the history of the Western world. By 1749 they had founded a congregation and within ten years they dedicated a synagogue. The Jews, like others in the colony, were given free entrance into any profession they wished. Moses Lindo, a Jewish merchant and broker, settled in Charleston and raised indigo, a plant from which a blue dye is made. He was appointed Surveyor-General of Indigo for the entire colony and had much to do with its economic development.

* * *

By the time of the American Revolution, there were five Jewish settlements in the United States. They were located in the colonies that had shown the greatest liberalism toward minorities. In order of their founding they were New York, Newport, Charleston, Savannah and Philadelphia. Jews were in a variety of jobs. Many were merchants and traders. Excluded from land ownership and crafts in Europe, forced by persecution to move from place to place, Jews had friends and relatives throughout Europe, South America, and the West Indies with whom they maintained mercantile connections. They exported America's furs, flax, rice, fish, sugar, and indigo. Like other merchants of the time, some Jewish merchants participated in the slave trade. Not all Jews, however, were merchants. Some were doctors, manual laborers, shopkeepers, watchmakers, shoemakers, silversmiths, wigmakers, bakers, candlemakers or butchers. They participated in the growth of the Colonies in many different capacities.

Massachusetts

In Colonies other than those already mentioned, the situation was quite different. Where there was no room for dissident minorities, where religious zeal was so intense that it could stand no competition, Jews, Catholics and other minorities fared poorly. Puritan Massachusetts, for example, was so inhospitable that no meaningful Jewish community was to be found there. Despite its heavy reliance on the Hebrew Bible, it abhorred Jews and all other different sects. Puritans came to America seeking to worship as they chose, not to grant that freedom to others. Their intolerance drove out Roger Williams and Anne Hutchinson, who were key figures in the founding of Rhode Island. It is therefore not surprising that only a few Jews appear in the early records of the Bay Colony. One was Judah Monis, the first Jew to receive a degree from an American university. He was awarded an honorary Master of Arts degree from Harvard in 1720. But the illiberality of Massachusetts led him to convert to Christianity two years later, whereupon he was appointed to the Harvard faculty as an instructor in Hebrew. Some years later the university published his Hebrew gram-

William Bradford his Booke

A° 1652

אין חכמה ואין תבונה ואין עצה
לנגד יהוה

There no wisdom, neither
nor nsel, against the Lord

Governor William Bradford of Massachusetts was a student of the Hebrew language. This is the first page of his Hebrew lesson book.

Aaron Lopez, distinguished citizen of Newport, Rhode Island.

mar. Eighty years elapsed before the next Jew was enrolled there.

Biblical Influence

Even though there was no Jewish community in Massachusetts at this time, there was an important Jewish presence. Long before Jews were permitted to settle there, the Hebrew Scriptures had profoundly influenced colonial thought in many ways and left a permanent impression on American culture. The Puritan theocracy was clearly modeled after that of ancient Israel, as Bay Colony leaders carefully chose from both Biblical and English legal sources. They synthesized scriptural precedent with the complex heritage of English law and adapted both to fit the daily requirements of life in New England. Puritans derived from their study of the Hebrew Bible the conviction that God was the only true King, which justified their establishment of a theocracy governed by His deputies as well as the belief that all men were equally humble before Him, a concept preserved in the American ideal of respect for the dignity and worth of the individual. Puritans were convinced that like the ancient Israelites, they too were God's chosen people, bound by the covenant between God and men. Governor Winthrop, who led the first settlers in Massachusetts, assured them, "If we keep this covenant we shall find that the God of Israel is among us, but if we deal falsely with our God . . . we shall be consumed out of the good land He has promised."

The Puritans looked upon themselves as the new Israelites who had escaped Pharaoh across the Red Sea. Mosaic Law, their unchallengeable authority, was one of the sources for early New England legal codes. It was meant to guide all future legal activities, an attitude clearly seen in such early documents as the Mayflower Compact and the Salem Covenant. In 1641 a Body of Liberties was enacted in New England. Of its forty-eight laws, forty-six were drawn from the Hebrew Bible.

Early New England chose its magistrates, drafted its laws,

and conducted general legislative procedures in large measure according to Scripture. In matters of government, the Reverend John Davenport of New Haven, for example, was determined to "drive things . . . as near to the precept and pattern of Scripture as they could be driven." The preface to the Massachusetts Legal Code of 1648, the Western hemisphere's first modern legal code, reiterates the preëminence of God's law:

> As soon as God had set up a Political Government among his people Israel he gave them a body of laws for judgment both in civil and criminal causes. These were brief and fundamental principles, yet withal so full and comprehensive as out of them clear deductions were to be drawn to particular cases in future times.

The Puritans also based much of their religion and daily lives on the Hebrew Bible. Their names were often Biblical and like Jews they observed the Sabbath and other holidays from sundown to sundown. Like Orthodox Jews today they refrained from all work on the Sabbath. Their feasts often developed from Jewish holidays. Thanksgiving was patterned after the Jewish harvest celebration of *Sukkot*. While Puritan practice did not always derive from Jewish precedent, Puritans were fully aware of the many similarities between their religion and Judaism. They denied sacramental status to the minister, who, like the rabbi, derived his spiritual authority from his personal piety, and his knowledge of God's law which was accessible to all. Neither was a member of any priesthood. Each held his position by dint of ability and strength of character. Other aspects of Puritan religion, such as congregational autonomy and the absence of an episcopal hierarchy, also paralleled Jewish experience, although they derived more immediately from the Protestant Reformation.

The veneration of the Hebrew Scriptures was also reflected in educational practice. Hebrew was a major subject at Harvard as early as 1655. Morning prayers included a verse from the Bible in Hebrew and commencement exercises included an oration in Hebrew. At Yale the study of Hebrew was mandatory, "essential to a gentleman's education." The language was even required of small children in some public schools.

The lives of some early New England leaders also reveal a Biblical influence. Many were ardent Hebraists. Cotton Mather, the great Puritan leader, began studying Hebrew at the age of twelve and mastered it in college. He also studied the Talmud* and wrote a six-volume history of the Jews. He and the Puritans were greatly impressed by Jewish respect for learning. Mather commented, "In every town among Jews there was a school, whereat children were taught the reading of the law. . . ." Roger Williams, the founder of Rhode Island, and Thomas Hooker, the liberal leader of Connecticut, studied Scripture in Hebrew.

The ancient Hebrew Commonwealth exerted far more influence on early America than the handful of Jewish settlers who made their way to the Colonies. The historian W.E.H. Lecky was correct in observing that "Hebraic mortar cemented the foundations of American democracy." Roger Williams, for example, proclaimed the Hebrew Bible the basis for his new theory of religious freedom. The people were the source of political authority. God had not ordained that men should control the conscience of other men.

Seventeenth-century New England's religious and political attitudes provided a backdrop for eighteenth-century political concepts. For the leaders of the American Revolution, the Hebrew Commonwealth was undeniable evidence that "Rebellion to tyrants is obedience to God." The New England clergy, often in the forefront of the drive for independence from England, frequently referred to the condemnation of human monarchy in I Samuel and quoted Moses, Joshua, Samuel and various Judges and Prophets to prove that God was the only true King. Political pamphleteers drew largely

* A vast body of Jewish literature consisting of explanations, interpretations, discussions and conclusions about Jewish life and knowledge, based on the Bible. To Jews, it is second in importance only to the Bible itself. The word "Talmud" derives from the Hebrew root, "to learn."

on Biblical sources. None was more effective than Tom Paine, who wrote in *Common Sense:*

> . . . . . exalting one man so greatly above the rest cannot . . . be defended on the authority of scripture; for the will of the Almighty as declared by Gideon, and the prophet Samuel expressly disapproves of government by kings.

No less attracted to Scriptural sources was the pious Pennsylvania Quaker who chose for the Liberty Bell the words from Leviticus (25:10), "Proclaim liberty throughout all the land unto all the inhabitants thereof," which prophetically rang true a quarter of a century later when the Bell tolled the Declaration of Independence.

Patriots found many democratic principles in Hebrew Scriptures. Moses, immediately after crossing the Red Sea, separated religion, state, and the military and delegated authority to leaders chosen by the people. Judges were selected solely on the basis of merit. In Canaan, Joshua was confirmed by the people as their chief executive, and was in time succeeded by a series of fourteen judges, selected by the people. The ancient Hebrews also elected a senate (Sanhedrin) of seventy-one elders which exercised legislative and judicial functions. For many of the nation's early political leaders the natural equality of men was as evident in the laws of Moses as it was in the Declaration of Independence.

Virginia and Maryland

New England was not the only area inhospitable to Jews. In Virginia, where the Church of England was entrenched and its clergy closely tied to the Crown, no significant Jewish community emerged. Nor did one appear in Maryland which was unique among the Colonies, in that it was founded as a haven for Catholics, one of the most persecuted peoples in the English-speaking world in the eighteenth century. Maryland law excluded from the colony anyone not professing a belief in Jesus Christ, which meant that no professing Jew was admitted. Any Jew who settled there had to conceal his religion. Accurate records of Jews in Maryland, therefore, do not exist. In 1649 the General Assembly of Maryland passed "An Act Concerning Religion," which provided that anyone who denied Jesus and the Holy Trinity, or spoke against it, would be put to death and forfeit all his property. Accordingly, Jacob Lumbrozo, a Jewish physician from Lisbon, was charged with "uttering words of blasphemy against our Blessed Savior Jesus Christ" during a debate with a visiting Christian missionary. However, he was not put to death. His case is the only known prosecution of a Jew for that offense in American history.

When Maryland reverted to the crown in 1691, Catholics and Jews were both oppressed. Jews were discouraged from settling in the colony, ineligible to vote, hold office, or worship in public, and like Catholics, they were subject to a head tax of £200. No permanent Jewish settlement developed in Maryland until the Revolution, when the city of Baltimore began to attract Jewish settlers. Maryland was one of the last states in the Union to relax its discriminatory laws against Jews. They lingered until 1826 when the "Maryland Jew Bill" finally eliminated them.

* * *

On the eve of the American Revolution, about three million Americans were living along the Atlantic seaboard. Perhaps two thousand were Jewish. Until the mid-nineteenth century, Jewish migration to America amounted to no more than a trickle. In those Colonies in which liberal charters and tolerant governments welcomed them, Jews settled and participated in the life of the community. In Colonies where adherence to one sect was required, Jews and other minorities stayed away. The major Jewish centers of early Colonial times were New York, Rhode Island, Pennsylvania, Georgia, and South Carolina, and even in these Colonies Jews tended to keep together as in "Jews' Alley." They had escaped the horrors of the Inquisition, and life was dramatically improved, but they had by no means been completely accepted in

America. Most were not wealthy. They insisted on living according to the teachings of Judaism, and as in the case of Asser Levy, stubbornly fought for full civil rights. Few ever returned to the countries from which they had emigrated.

TO THE TEACHER:

The association of Jews with Columbus should not be viewed in isolation from its historical context. The fact that Jews came with Columbus as *Marranos* (secret Jews) says more about the Inquisition and life in fifteenth and sixteenth century Spain than it does about the contributions of the Jews. In general teachers should not over-emphasize the contributions of minority figures. In the case of Luis de Torres, for example, it is more important to understand the reason for his decision to remain in America than it is to laud the fact that it was a Jew who first settled in the Western hemisphere. The fact that the Lopez and Rivera families of Newport, Rhode Island, could openly worship as Jews after eight generations as *Marranos,* is far more significant in understanding the nature of civic equality in that colony than is the obvious success of Aaron Lopez or Jacob Rodriguez Rivera. Moreover, mention of a man's religion is generally unnecessary and should be avoided unless, as in the case of de Torres, it helps explain his role in history, or as in the case of Lopez and Rivera, it sheds light on the society in which he lived.

Rejection of Jewish settlers in parts of Colonial America underscores the fact that America was not always a land of religious tolerance and equality, notwithstanding the widespread and inaccurate portrayal of the early Colonies as havens of religious liberty. Separation of church and state had to be achieved. Much material in this chapter reflects not only on this struggle, but on the diversity of the original thirteen Colonies, among which there existed conflicting views about the place of religious dissidents. Puritans, for example, did not come to America to establish religious liberty. They came to perpetuate their own brand of orthodoxy, and were exceedingly intolerant of others. The absence of a Jewish community in Colonial Massachusetts illuminates this fact.

However, though few Jews were to be found in Massachusetts, a Hebrew presence is discernible. The principal theme here is the impact of the Hebrew Bible on early American thought and its lasting influence on American culture. In this connection, this chapter suggests the possible indebtedness of the colonists to the Hebrew Bible as a source for such concepts and institutions as the republican form of government; the separation of the executive, legislative, and judicial functions of government; separation of church and state; and civil and religious equality.

The chapter also bears on the concept of America as a nation of immigrants in which ethnic and religious variations were present from the earliest days as contrasted to the more homogeneous population of other nations. Teachers are cautioned that Jews were not the only victims of religious intolerance and persecution in Colonial America. So were Catholics, Lutherans, Quakers, and others.

The limited acquisition of civil and religious equality by Jews is an explicit theme throughout this chapter. It is especially clear in the material concerning Jews in New Amsterdam. But teachers should avoid presenting only the positive aspects of minority history. What Jews did not do, and why, is equally important. The absence of meaningful Jewish communities in early Massachusetts, Virginia, and Maryland is as important to the study of Colonial intolerance as their presence is to understanding the principles upon which Rhode Island was founded. The fact that Jews first voted in America in 1703, in South Carolina, reflects on the liberality of that colony much more than it does on the role of the Jews. Viewed in terms of interaction with the larger society, the role of any ethnic or religious minority, whether positive or negative, sheds light on American history as well as on the minority groups being considered.

DISCUSSION QUESTIONS AND STUDENT ACTIVITIES

1. Explain this statement: In many ways Jews in Spain helped make Columbus' voyage possible. Include the role of Jews who provided navigation information and tools, knowledge of astronomy, financial assistance, and who were members of Columbus' crew.
2. Pretend that you are Luis de Torres. Write your family in Spain justifying your decision to remain in the New World.
3. Some scholars have suggested that Columbus was Jewish (a *Marrano*). Prepare a report to either substantiate or refute this.
4. The last boatload of Jews exiled from Spain in 1492 sailed from the same port and on the same tide as Columbus. Prepare an imaginary dialogue between a sailor on the deck of Columbus's ship and a Jew whose ship lay moored nearby. What fears and anxieties might each have expressed? What common interests might they have shared?
5. Jews generally lived harmoniously with the Moslems in Spain and Babylonia. Do a research project to find what Judaism and the Moslem faith have in common. Begin with their common origin in the Book of Genesis, 21:9-21 which tells the story of Ishmael and Hagar. How do Jewish-Arab relations compare with Jewish-Christian relations during the last 2,000 years?
6. By 1630 *Marranos* in Brazil were liberated from Portuguese rule by the Dutch and were able to practice Judaism openly. In 1654 Brazil was recaptured by the Portuguese and the Jews were unable to remain nor could they become secret Jews (*Marranos*) again. What metaphor might be useful in describing their plight? You might say they were like whales stranded on a beach, like fish out of water, or like a groundhog, who, after leaving his tunnel, finds it has collapsed. What others can you think of? In what ways do they illustrate the position of the Brazilian Jews? In what ways do they

not? (For further information on the use of metaphor in teaching, refer to *Making It Strange,* Harper and Row, New York, 1968, and *The Metaphorical Way,* Porpoise Books, Cambridge, 1971. Both are by W. J. Gordon.)

7. Role-play the situation of the twenty-three Jews who arrived in New Amsterdam in 1654. Carefully select players for Peter Stuyvesant, Asser Levy, and the three or four others who might have been prominent in the group. Let the dramatization center around Stuyvesant's opposition to the Jews. The actors should research the material well in advance, but the role play should be improvisational. Stop the action after a minute or two. Let the class comment on how well it is going, and make specific suggestions to the actors before the role-play resumes. The teacher should sidecoach but should instruct the players not to respond directly to him, only to incorporate his suggestions into their acting. He might say, for example, "How does Stuyvesant feel?" "Is he annoyed?" "Let his face show annoyance." "Asser Levy! Are you angry? Show it in your posture. Use your hands." (An excellent book on this technique is *Improvisation for the Theater,* by Viola Spolin, Northwestern University Press, Evanston, Illinois, 1963.)
8. Have thirteen students each study the attitude of a different colony toward Jews and other minorities. Have the students arrange themselves in a semicircle in front of the room, with the most liberal colony at one end and the least liberal at the other. Have each make a statement about his colony with respect to its attitude toward the arrival of Jewish and other minority immigrants. Allow the rest of the class to challenge their order and question their statements. Signs or labels might be helpful. A Polaroid photo of the final arrangement might add to the interest.
9. Write or visit the Touro Synagogue in Newport, Rhode Island. (It is now a national monument.) Ask for the free brochure about the synagogue and prices of picture

postcards and additional literature published by the Newport Historical Society.

10. Read the poem by Longfellow, "The Jewish Cemetery at Newport." (Excerpts are in Pessin, *History of the Jews in America,* p. 64, and Levinger, *History of the Jews in the United States,* p. 75. See Basic Bibliography.) What prompted Longfellow to write this poem? What was his point of view? What does he mean by the metaphor, "Ishmaels and Hagars of mankind"?
11. Write an imaginary exchange of letters between a Jew of Newport, and a Jew who attempted to settle in Massachusetts. Base their words on your knowledge of how these colonies treated Jews.
12. Assume you are a Jew who came from England to Georgia in the early eighteenth century. Using only the first person, write your story. How many others came with you? What kinds of people did you find there? How did they react to you and you to them? How did James Oglethorpe treat you? What rights did you enjoy?
13. Write a research report on the early history of the Jews in your particular city or state. There are numerous local histories of Jews which should be helpful.
14. Puritans often thought of themselves as latter-day Israelites, fleeing Pharaoh. Read the story of the Exodus in the Hebrew Bible. Compare it to the Puritan "exodus" to America. In what respects are these migrations similar or different? Formulate some generalizations about migrations of people from one land to another.
15. Explain this contradiction: The Puritans relied heavily on Hebrew Scriptures and the Jewish religion in the formation of their own laws and way of life, yet they did not welcome Jews into their colony.
16. Find a good book about Jewish holidays and festivals. (See *Your Neighbor Celebrates* published by the Anti-Defamation League of B'nai B'rith.) Also locate a good history of the Puritans. Write a report on how Puritan festivals derived from Jewish celebrations. An example

is Thanksgiving which is related to the Hebrew celebration of *Sukkot*. How many others are there?

17. Puritanism resembled Judaism in that, among other things, both denied sacramental status to the minister or rabbi and both were congregationally governed. Visit a synagogue to learn how Judaism views the rabbi today, and how it is organized and governed. What role does the rabbi play? Who is in charge? How is the synagogue a model of organizational democracy? How does it compare to your church in this respect? What is the role of women?
18. Look up the history of the Liberty Bell. Report on why the Jubilee inscription, "Proclaim liberty throughout all the land unto all the inhabitants thereof," from Leviticus 25:10, was chosen. Can you suggest other mottoes for the Liberty Bell? How would they be appropriate?
19. Look up Samuel's advice (1 Samuel 8:10-19) to the children of Israel on choosing a king and Gideon's words on monarchy (Judges 8:22-23). How did Thomas Paine use these sources in *Common Sense?* (Refer to *The Complete Writings of Thomas Paine,* edited by Philip S. Foner, Citadel Press, New York, 1969, Vol. 1, pp. 10-12, or any good collection of Paine's writings.)
20. What did the historian W. E. H. Lecky mean in observing that, "Hebraic mortar cemented the foundations of American democracy?"

BIBLIOGRAPHY

Alexander, Lloyd, *The Flagship Hope: Aaron Lopez* (Jewish Publication Society, Philadelphia, 1960). The story of a Portuguese *Marrano* who became a leading Jew in Colonial America. An excellent fictional biography for junior high school students.

Duff, Charles, *The Truth About Columbus and the Discovery of America* (Jarrolds, London, 1957). A very detailed, thorough study of the life and voyages of Columbus.

Chapter 3 is an outstanding analysis of the role of Jews in the discovery of America. The author goes far deeper into the subject than do other major writers on Columbus. Recommended for teachers and the most capable high school students doing research. Pages 260-263 contain a brief bibliography concerning Columbus and the discovery of America.

Friedman, Lee M., *Jewish Pioneers and Patriots* (Jewish Publication Society, Philadelphia, 1955). Particularly useful are: chapter 5 (Columbus); 8 (Cotton Mather); 11 (Asser Levy); 18 (the Campanel family of New England); 21 (the Touro family); 26 (the Lopez family and the New England whaling industry). An interesting book. Recommended for teachers and capable high school students.

Friedman, Lee M., *Pilgrims in a New Land* (Jewish Publication Society, Philadelphia, 1948). Among many important topics developed in this book, chapter 1 provides a very useful discussion of the Biblical antecedents of early America. Chapter 13 discusses the theory that the Indians were descended from the ten lost tribes of Israel. Well written and very readable. Recommended for teachers and high school students.

Gaer, Joseph and Siegal, Ben, *The Puritan Heritage: America's Roots in the Bible* (New American Library, New York, 1964, Mentor paperback). This is, perhaps, the best book in the field. It contains scholarly, fascinating discussions of the influence of the Bible on the early Puritan settlements, government, law, education, and literature, and a most intriguing chapter on the Biblical and Talmudic relationship to the practice of medicine and personal hygiene in early America. Suitable for better than average high school students and highly recommended for teachers. The bibliography on pages 227-246 is outstanding. This is a must for anyone seeking a full understanding of America's Biblical roots.

Goodman, Abram V., *American Overture* (Jewish Publication Society, Philadelphia, 1947). The story of expanding Jewish rights in Colonial times. Deals with the history of the Jewish community in a number of Colonies. An academic treatment, primarily suited for teachers and above-average high school students doing research.

Huhner, Leon, *Jews in Colonial and Revolutionary Times* (Gertz Brothers, New York, 1959). Another scholarly work about Jews in Colonial America. A collection of articles on a variety of topics. The book is academically sound, well-documented, and recommended for teachers and better than average high school students.

Ish Kishor, Sulamith, *American Promise, A History of the Jews in the New World* (Behrman House, New York, 1947) is a general history of the Jews in America. Suitable for junior high school students. Chapters 1-6 and 8 are particularly relevant to this chapter. Because it is simply written, this book should be useful for older students with reading difficulties.

Lebeson, Anita Libman, *Pilgrim People* (Harper & Bros., New York, 1950). A history of American Jewry. Poorly organized and sometimes confusing. It tends to ramble and concern itself with petty detail, but is nonetheless very informative. Chapter 2 deals with Jews who were associated with the voyages of Columbus. Recommended for teachers and high school students.

Levinger, Elma Ehrlich, *Jewish Adventures in America* (Bloch Publishing Co., New York, 1954). This is a simple biographical survey of Jews in the history and development of America. The author divides the material into three major sections, early, middle, and modern. Section 1 parallels this chapter, concluding with the American Revolution. Recommended for junior high readers. The book is carefully written and because each line is separated by a larger amount of space than is usual, it might also be useful for older students with reading difficulties.

Levinger, Lee J., *A History of the Jews in the United States* (Union of American Hebrew Congregations, New York, 1961). Chapter 2 deals with Jews who assisted Columbus. Chapters 3-7 cover Jewish Colonial settlements. Chapter 10 summarizes Spanish-Jewish immigration. The information is detailed but suitable for teachers and junior high and high school students.

Marcus, Jacob R., *The Colonial American Jew, 1492-1776* (Wayne State University Press, Detroit, 1970). A three-volume history of the pre-Revolutionary Jewish community by the dean of American-Jewish historians. Chapter 2, "Marranos and New Christians in the Spanish Americas," includes an excellent discussion of whether or not Columbus was Jewish. Chapter 3 details Jewish life in Brazil until the fall of Recife in 1654. Chapters 9 through 15 provide a wealth of material on Jewish settlement in the various colonies under the Dutch and the British. Chapter 63 discusses the teaching of Hebrew to non-Jews. Recommended for teachers and superior high school students doing research.

Marcus, Jacob R., *Early American Jewry* (Jewish Publication Society, Philadelphia, 1951-53). An in-depth but very readable examination of Jewish life in the seventeenth and eighteenth centuries. Volume I deals with the Jews of New York, New England, and Canada from 1649 to 1794. Volume II deals with Jews of Pennsylvania and the South from 1655 to 1790. Recommended for teachers and very capable high school students doing research.

Rosenbaum, Jeannette W., *Myer Myers, Goldsmith, 1723-1795* (Jewish Publication Society, Philadelphia, 1954). This biography of a little-known Colonial Jewish craftsman gives balance to any study of American-Jewish history. It provides, in addition, an excellent picture of the Colonial world. Recommended primarily for high school students.

Roth, Cecil, *A History of the Marranos* (Jewish Publication Society of America, Philadelphia, 1932). This is a thorough, scholarly work providing a great deal of material on an important aspect of Jewish history—the *Marranos*. The first half of the book deals with the Inquisition and is the part most relevant to this chapter. Recommended for teachers and advanced high school students.

St. John, Robert, *Jews, Justice and Judaism* (Doubleday, New York, 1969). The first five chapters cover the Colonial scene. Interestingly written and informative. Recommended for teachers and high school students in search of a painless introduction to this material.

Straus, Oscar, *The Origins of the Republican Form of Government in the United States of America* (G. P. Putnam's Sons, New York, 1926). A classic. Oscar Strauss was probably the first to write about the impact of the Hebrew Bible on Colonial America and of the influence of the Hebrew Commonwealth on the establishment of a Republican form of government in the United States. In this short book (151 pages) he gives a thorough and provocative analysis of these ideas. The book may not be available in small libraries, but is well worth tracking down. Suitable for research by high school students and teachers.

Wise, William, *Silversmith of Old New York, Myer Myers* (Jewish Publication Society, Philadelphia, 1959). The life and adventures of an early-American Jewish silversmith. Myers was a friend of Paul Revere and his biography illuminates Jewish family life during the Colonial era. A good biography for junior high school readers.

AUDIO-VISUAL MATERIALS

Isaac Abravanel: Scholar and Statesman, a filmstrip produced by Samuel Grand, 1966. 41 frames, color, includes 2 copies of teacher's guide. Sponsored and distributed by the Commission on Jewish Education, Union of American Hebrew Congregations, 838 Fifth Ave., New York, N. Y. 10021. A biographical study of the famous fifteenth-century Jewish-Portuguese leader and his contributions to Jewish religious thought. Does not adequately explain the high position Abravanel held in Spain and Portugal during a period of general anti-Semitism, nor does it give satisfactory background for the expulsion of the Jews in 1492. However, it is informative and worth using. Recommended primarily for high school audiences.

The Jews Settle in New Amsterdam—1654, a filmstrip produced by Victor Kayfetz Productions, Inc., 1952. 37 frames, color distributed by the Union of American Hebrew Congregations, 838 Fifth Ave., New York, N. Y. 10021. This prize-winning filmstrip describes the first group of Jewish settlers in America and their struggle for equality. Technical quality is excellent; the script is interesting and the story continuity uniform throughout. Suitable for junior high and high school audiences.

Menasseh Ben Israel: Man of Dreams and Deeds, a filmstrip produced by Samuel Grand, 1966. 39 frames, color, includes 2 copies of teacher's guide. Sponsored and distributed by the Commission on Jewish Education, Union of American Hebrew Congregations, 838 Fifth Ave., New York, N. Y. 10021. This informative filmstrip tells the life story of Menasseh Ben Israel, who helped secure permission for the Jews to settle in New Amsterdam in 1654. Recommended for high school audiences.

The World of Rembrandt, a kinescope of an Eternal Light television program, produced by the Jewish Theological Seminary of America in cooperation with NBC-TV, 1968, 30 minutes, black and white and color. Distributed by the National Academy for Adult Jewish Studies of the United Synagogue of America, 218 East 70th St., New York, N. Y. 10021. This is a documentary filmed on location in Amsterdam featuring works of this great artist. Most pertinent to this chapter are scenes dealing with the history of the Jews in Holland. The film is not well organized, but nonethless helps create background for a study of the Jews in New Amsterdam in the Colonial period. Recommended for high school groups.

Chicago's memorial to George Washington. Haym Salomon stands to the left of Washington and Robert Morris to his right.

CHAPTER II

REVOLUTION AND CIVIC EQUALITY

*

IMPORTANT EVENTS

1776-86	The Anglican Church is disestablished in all colonies in which it had been tax-supported.
1786	Virginia passes the world's first law to establish religious freedom.
1787	The Constitution of the United States bars religious tests for federal office.
1791	The Bill of Rights prohibits Congressional establishment of religion.
1833	Massachusetts becomes the last state to disestablish the Church.
1868	The Fourteenth Amendment protects privileges and immunities of U.S. Ciitzens and establishes "due process clause."

Jews in the American Revolution

On the eve of the American Revolution, most American Jews chose the patriot cause and were soon caught up in the movement that culminated in the War of Independence. Since many were merchants, they were active in the protest movements and non-importation resolutions prior to the fighting. Like other Americans, they resented British attempts to tighten imperial control over the Colonies after the French and Indian War. When fighting did erupt, Jews were in the Continental Army, both as officers and common soldiers. Lieutenant-Colonel Isaac Franks of New York fought at the Battle of Long Island, and his cousin, Lieutenant-Colonel David Salisbury Franks, was one of Benedict Arnold's two leading aides on the retreat from Canada early in the war.

Lieutenant-Colonel Solomon Bush of Philadelphia was Deputy Adjutant-General of the Pennsylvania State Militia. A heavily Jewish South Carolina company earned a reputation for valiant service, particularly in defense of Charleston against the British. A few Jews even came from Europe to fight. A Frenchman, Benjamin Nones, left his vineyards in Bordeaux and served under General Pulaski, then under DeKalb, and finally as a major under Lafayette and Washington. He helped defend Savannah and was cited by General Pulaski for valor in action.

Jews supported the Revolution in other ways. Aaron Lopez, the prominent New England shipper, donated much of his fortune to the Continental cause. He and other Jewish shipowners armed their vessels with cannon and sent them out to prey on British shipping, inflicting considerable damage. In Philadelphia, Haym Salomon, Paymaster-General for the French forces and later official broker to the Continental Congress, floated loans, endorsed government notes, and invested most of his own money in government bonds which proved to be worthless. He equipped entire military units from his personal funds and even paid the salaries of some revolutionary leaders when the treasury ran dry. He advanced money to Thomas Jefferson, James Madison, James Monroe, and many other delegates to the Continental Congress in Philadelphia, consistently refusing interest when and if they repaid their loans.

Mordecai Sheftall of Georgia was chairman of Savannah's Parochial Committee, the *de facto* government the radicals had set up to help run the state. He later served as Commissary-General, supplying arms and food to the soldiers of Georgia and South Carolina. He helped in the defense of Savannah, and following the war was awarded a grant of land by a grateful government.

A few American Jews supported the British. The most prominent was David Franks, probably a relative of Isaac and David Salisbury Franks. He was a leading Philadelphia merchant and politician who supported George III, supplying

Isaac Franks (1759-1822), revolutionary soldier, painted by Gilbert Stuart.

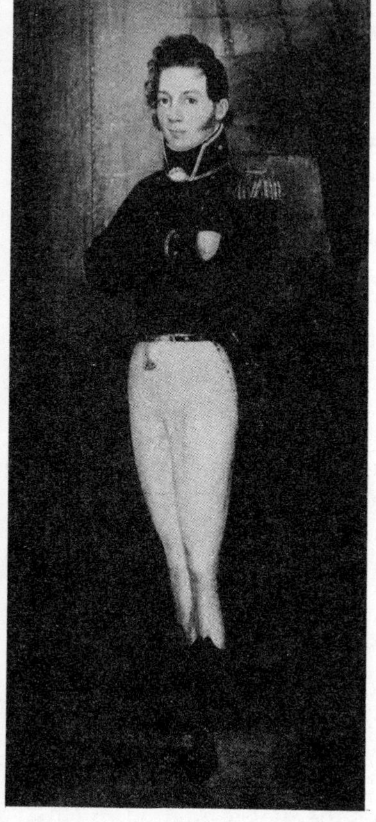

Uriah Phillips Levy (1792-1862), fighting naval man and admirer of Thomas Jefferson. He helped abolish corporal punishment in the United States Navy, where he rose to the highest rank, that of flag officer or commodore.

the British troops until he was imprisoned by the Colonial government and expelled from Philadelphia. In Newport, Isaac Hart, prominent merchant and leader of the Jewish community, refused to take an oath to support the patriots, and, as happened to other Loyalists during this period, he was beaten to death by an angry mob.

In politics Jews were insignificant since holding public office was still forbidden them almost everywhere. An exception was Francis Salvador, a wealthy South Carolina planter, who was sent as deputy to the colony's Provincial Assembly in Charleston, and in 1774 was elected to the South Carolina General Assembly. He died defending Charleston against the British.

The War of 1812

In the War of 1812 Jews again fought side by side with other Americans. A number of Jewish names are reminiscent of the Revolution, among them several grandsons of Mordecai Sheftall and a son of Haym Salomon. At the Battle of New Orleans, Judah Touro, son of Newport's first cantor, achieved fame under General Andrew Jackson. Commodore Uriah Phillips Levy, the highest ranking Jewish naval officer of his day, was captured by the British during the War of 1812, and subsequently devoted much of his career to a crusade which culminated in a law abolishing corporal punishment in the United States Navy. An ardent admirer of Thomas Jefferson, he was for many years the owner of Monticello, Jefferson's home in Virginia, which was preserved as a national shrine as a result of Levy's efforts.

The Meaning of the Revolution

There were very few Jews in the new nation. Yet our comprehension of the meaning of the American Revolution for all persons can be deepened by way of reference to the Jews, not because their numbers were large or their achievements major—they were not—but because the transformation which the Revolution effected in the civic condition of the Jews was particularly radical and allows us to grasp even more clearly its meaning for people in general.

Prior to the Revolution, the executive authority which ultimately governed the Colonies was lodged in an hereditary monarch. After the Revolution it was exercised by an elected president. In that change lies much of the meaning of the Revolution. The authority which justified an hereditary king and that which justifies an elected president are radically different. The king's authority, except insofar as it was limited by an elected parliament, in no way derived from the consent of the governed. The king could claim that his authority was inherited from his predecessors or that it derived from God, in which case he would be described as a "theocratic" ruler, a term which derives from the Greek words meaning "God" and "to govern."

With the king as God's deputy, the church usually supported him. The king, in turn, shared with the church some powers of government. Frequently, for example, the king acknowledged the right of the church to wield authority over his subjects in matters of belief, alms-giving, marriage and domestic relations, so that two governments coexisted, that of the king and that of the church. Each reinforced the other's authority. Characteristically, the oath of allegiance that is now purely secular in nature, was then underwritten by religious authority. The oath of allegiance to the King of England, for instance, required a person to swear "upon the true faith of a Christian."

The consequence of this arrangement, which prevailed with many local variations during the Middle Ages and to a lesser degree down to the American and French Revolutions, was to make of the Jews and of many other religious minorities outcasts in the kingdoms in which they lived. The Jew refused to accept the jurisdiction of the church. Since the church was connected with the state, the religious dissent of the Jew could be interpreted as an act of political disloyalty and as an attack on the authority of the crown as well, notwithstanding the fact that the Jew was admonished by the law of his own religion to be faithful to the government under whose protection he lived. Much the same was also true of other minorities. A minority Catholic population was suspect in a predominantly Protestant country and vice versa. The same was frequently true of dissident Protestants in a Protestant country. The state would attempt to impose conformity to the beliefs and practices of the church whose support it enjoyed. Civil war was frequently the result.

In the course of the American Revolution the theocratic claim was laid to rest. The king was replaced by an elected president who governed because he was authorized by the people to do so. Political authority was now democratic, a term that derives from two Greek words meaning "people" and "to govern." Governmental authority was no longer underwritten by religion. This change is evident in several provisions of the Constitution of the United States which provides in Article VI that "no religious test shall ever be required as a qualification to any office or public trust under the United States."

The colonists were thus enfranchised by the Revolution. They were no longer subjects, but citizens claiming and exercising the right to vote, subject, of course, to the prevailing restrictions of property, race and sex. The attainment of a civic identity, momentous enough in itself, was even more so for the Jews and other minorities, whose political loyalties had frequently been questioned. The Revolution made them citizens of a secular state, in which the religion of the individual was irrelevant. All minorities henceforth were full members of the civic and political community.

This transformation was eloquently expressed by George Washington. Shortly after he took office as President of the United States, the Jews of Newport sent him a letter of congratulations, expressing their happiness at living under the authority of a "government which to bigotry gives no sanction, to persecution no assistance . . ." Washington's reply incorporated the same phraseology:

> It is now no more that toleration is spoken of, as if it was by the indulgence of one class of people that another enjoyed the exercise of their inherent natural rights. For happily, the government of the United States, which gives to bigotry no sanction, to persecution no assistance, requires only that they who live under its protection should demean themselves as good citizens, in giving it on all occasions their effectual support.

Separation of Church and State

The American Revolution made equally momentous changes in the nature of the church. As long as the church remained a kind of state, supported by the king, the existence of two or more churches would mean that rivals fought for the allegiance of each subject, and for establishment as the only church. Such rivalry led to much bloodshed. This source of conflict was ended by the Revolution. The First Amendment to the Constitution provided that "Congress shall make no law respecting an establishment of religion or prohibiting the free exercise thereof." This meant that all churches were now transformed into purely voluntary associations of men and women which each citizen was free to join or not as he chose, without having his patriotism called into question. The centuries-old scourge of religious civil war was finally laid to rest.

Thus the American Revolution made for drastic changes in the way society was governed. Some were realized almost at once. Others, particularly the civic equality and religious liberty of some minorities and women, required a period of time before they were achieved. This was especially true in the matter of bringing existing colonial law into line with the principles inherent in the Revolution and affirmed in the Constitution. In the remainder of this chapter, this process is discussed in three stages. First, the colonial laws which mandated penalties against Jews and other minorities frequently went unenforced in practice, the more so the nearer the Revolution itself approached. Second, the Supreme

Court, by means of the due process clause of the Fourteenth Amendment, gradually made federal constitutional principles binding on the states. Third, over a period of time the states themselves gradually brought their constitutions and laws into conformity with the principles of the United States Constitution.

Colonial Laws

European prejudices and practices followed Jews to the American Colonies where they again faced discrimination. Jews were, in some cases, denied citizenship, the right to vote, the right to hold office, bear arms, or serve on juries. Their legal disabilities, however, were aimed not only against them specifically as Jews, but rather were a consequence of their position outside the established church, a position they shared with other dissenting groups. Almost from the start, however, such practices became anachronistic in America. The paucity of settlers in the Colonial wilderness meant that settlers were welcomed from wherever they came and the kind of society they produced differed sharply from that of the Old World, with its rigid class structure and social restrictions.

A tendency to ignore the legal disabilities of Jews was evident by the end of the seventeenth century and by the end of the eighteenth century was an established trend. In Massachusetts religious zeal declined as the founders died off and their children proved less inclined to the religious convictions of their parents. Change also sprang from the influence of the Enlightenment which altered fundamental concepts of human rights and dignity. During the eighteenth century religious diversity had become so characteristic of Colonial life that religious toleration was an accepted fact. Statutory restrictions against Jews were rarely repealed, as such, but broader attitudes frequently rendered them meaningless in practice. A live and let live attitude prevailed which suggests a much greater freedom of religion than a mere perusal of legal codes would indicate.

The legitimate place of Jews in the Colonies was recognized by an Act of Parliament in 1740 which exempted them from the religious clause, "upon the true faith of a Christian," in the naturalization oath. The oath persisted in England but the Act specifically exempted those in America "who profess the Jewish Religion." Jews in the Colonies had already advanced farther than their contemporaries in England or in any other part of the Western world.

Gradually Jews had acquired some civil and religious rights, but on the eve of the Revolution they were still a tiny minority in a society which maintained an established church and whose statute books contained numerous restrictions against them.

Constitutional Guarantees

Constitutional guarantees of freedom of religion were not automatically binding on the states in the new nation. Article VI, for example, stipulates that no person may be required to pass a religious test as a qualification for holding *federal* office. It does not prevent the *states* from imposing such a test for the holding of state office. The arrangement called federalism divided federal and state powers, and in some cases led to the denial of rights in a state that a citizen enjoyed on a national level. Therefore religious tests remained on the statute books of a number of states even after the adoption of the Constitution. Pennsylvania limited state office-holding to Christians and required a candidate to declare that he believed the Scriptures to be divinely inspired. New Jersey and North Carolina restricted office-holding to Protestants. The same is true of the First Amendment's guarantee of religious liberty and the prohibition of an establishment of religion. In 1833, in the case of *Barron* vs. *Baltimore,* the Supreme Court, led by John Marshall, ruled that the Bill of Rights limited the powers of the federal government but not the governments of the states. In 1845 the Supreme Court ruled more specifically that the Constitution did not protect citizens of states in their religious liberties. Similarly the

Constitution could not guarantee Jews the right to vote because the establishment of qualifications for voting was the prerogative of the individual state.

It was not until the adoption of the Fourteenth Amendment in 1868 that any significant attempt was made to limit the powers of the states. Following the Civil War, Congress, seeking to protect freed Negroes against arbitrary state action, passed the Fourteenth Amendment which subjected the states to the Bill of Rights. The Amendment provided that no state "shall make or enforce any law which shall abridge the privileges or immunities of citizens of the United States," and no state shall "deprive any person of life, liberty, or property, without due process of law."

However, the matter was not so easily resolved. In 1873 the Supreme Court decided that the Fourteenth Amendment did not extend all of the Bill of Rights to the states and left them nearly as unrestrained as before. In fact, for some time the members of the Supreme Court used the Fourteenth Amendment to write decisions favoring the development of big business and did not write interpretations supporting the rights of racial or religious minorities. It was not until 1923 that the Court ruled that due process included religious liberty. Again, in 1940 the Court held that religious freedom, as referred to in the First Amendment, is one of the liberties encompassed by the due process clause of the Fourteenth Amendment. At long last the Court had directed the states as well as the federal government to allow the free exercise of religion.

State Constitutions and Laws

Long before the 1923 Supreme Court decision, the states themselves had for many years been gradually amending their laws and constitutions or adopting new ones allowing for increased freedom of religion.

The First Amendment prohibited an "establishment of religion." However, a number of states supported established churches. One of the first states to disestablish the church was Virginia, where the loyalty of the Anglican clergy to the Crown made the established church a symbol of the imperial connection. In breaking with England, it became necessary to break with its church, as well. During the next ten years the Anglican Church was disestablished in all states in which it had been tax supported. In New England disestablishment of the church took much longer to achieve. The Congregational Church had originated in dissent and separation from Anglicanism and therefore had no ties with the English Crown. Many of the Congregational ministers championed the Revolution. As a consequence it was not until 1833 that Massachusetts severed the tie between church and state, the last state to do so, though discrimination had been substantially decreased since the first decade of the nineteenth century.

Quite apart from its prohibition of "an establishment of religion," the First Amendment protected religious liberty more directly still by forbidding Congress from interfering with the free exercise of religion. In this respect one of the states led the nation and even stole a march on the Constitution. Jefferson and Madison led the campaign which in 1786 culminated in the Virginia Statute of Religious Freedom. It declares:

> . . . no man shall be compelled to frequent or support any religious worship, place or ministry whatsoever . . . nor shall otherwise suffer on account of his religious opinions or beliefs; but that all men shall be free to profess, and by argument to maintain, their opinion in matters of religion, and that the same shall in no wise diminish, enlarge or affect their civil capacities.

This was probably the first such enactment in the world. Other states soon followed Virginia. By 1790 those whose liberal principles had made them receptive to Jewish settlers (New York, Georgia, Pennsylvania, and South Carolina) had passed similar laws.

Some states immediately abolished religious tests for public office. Others did not do so until well into the nineteenth century. In Maryland and North Carolina, for example, the number of Jews was small and the question of religious discrimination simply was not raised. Religious tests for public office continued in use, unchallenged, until the election of a Jew or the efforts of some conscientious Christian focused attention on the matter.

The case of Jacob Henry, of North Carolina, is an example of a discriminatory law being circumvented to conform to more liberal attitudes. In 1809 Henry was reëlected to the state House of Commons, but was challenged on the grounds that he was a Jew, a violation of the state requirement that all officials must be Protestants and accept the divine authority of the Christian Bible. He delivered an eloquent speech in his own defense and was aided in the debate by two prominent Catholics who were as much disturbed as he by the religious test. He was permitted to retain his seat by a legal subterfuge which avoided any change in the law. In 1835 the requirement was altered with respect to Catholics, but Jews, at least in theory, were not granted that equality until the religious test was abolished by a new state constitution in 1868.

A similar situation prevailed in Maryland, where, as early as the seventeenth century, a Toleration Act had discriminated against Jews. It was under that act that Dr. Jacob Lumbrozo had been charged with blasphemy. The Maryland Constitution of 1776 was hardly an improvement. It required "a declaration of belief in the Christian religion" to be eligible for state office. A petition by Jews in 1797 produced no relief, nor did numerous subsequent petitions. In 1818 Thomas Kennedy, a Scotch-Presbyterian immigrant and member of the state legislature, at considerable political risk, took an interest in the question. His repeated efforts culminated in passage of the so-called "Maryland Jew Bill" in 1826, which removed the offensive clause from the state constitution. Kennedy's attitude was remarkable considering that he represented a constituency entirely without Jews. "There are no Jews

SKETCH

OF

PROCEEDINGS IN THE

Legislature of Maryland,

DECEMBER SESSION, 1818,

ON WHAT IS COMMONLY CALLED

The Jew Bill;

CONTAINING

THE REPORT OF THE COMMITTEE

APPOINTED BY THE HOUSE OF DELEGATES

"To consider the justice and expediency of extending to those persons professing the Jewish Religion, the same privileges that are enjoyed by Christians:"

TOGETHER WITH

The Bill reported by the Committee,

AND

THE SPEECHES

OF

THOMAS KENNEDY, Esq. OF *WASHINGTON COUNTY*,

AND

H. M. BRACKENRIDGE, Esq. OF BALTIMORE CITY.

Baltimore:

PRINTED BY JOSEPH ROBINSON,

Circulating Library, corner of Market and Belvidere-streets.

1819

The report on the debate in December 1818 of the bill to grant equal rights to Jews in Maryland, introduced many times by Thomas Kennedy before it was finally passed in 1826.

in the country from which I come, nor have I the slightest acquaintance with any Jew in the world . . ." he stated, but "a religious test can never be productive of any good effect. . . ." He typified a growing number of Americans for whom abolition of religious tests for public office was an essential element in the concept of religious liberty.

By the end of the Jacksonian period most traces of privileged churches had disappeared. A few religious disabilities remained for Jews and other minorities until after the Civil War, but with few exceptions were not enforced. A generally friendly attitude toward Jews prevailed, even if the public was sometimes slow in correcting discriminatory legislation which lingered from an earlier day.

* * *

While Jews in America struggled to bring the law into conformity with actual practice, their counterparts in Europe were still far behind. In 1740 Parliament had exempted Colonial Jews from a religious clause in the naturalization oath; but the clause remained in England. In 1790 France emancipated its Jews, but even then the French looked to America, noting that the word "toleration," smacking too closely of sufferance rather than equality, had already been rejected there. Elsewhere the armies of the French Republic liberated Jews from the ghettos in the lands they conquered. But their gains were short-lived. The Congress of Vienna quickly erased them, providing the impetus for thousands of German immigrants to come to America later in the century. In central and eastern Europe Jews still lived in the Middle Ages, deprived of elemental human rights which American Jews took for granted. In America, where the European heritage of prejudice and discrimination had never taken firm root, Jews worshipped as they pleased, lived where they wished, followed any trade or profession they chose, and attended schools and universities along with other citizens.

TO THE TEACHER:

The diversity of Jewish participation in the Revolutionary War and the War of 1812 should be emphasized for it refutes the long-standing stereotype of the Jews as a clannish, homogeneous people. Even at this early date there were Jewish Radicals and Jewish Loyalists, Jewish merchants and Jewish artisans, Jewish enlisted men and Jewish officers.

In dealing with this early material, teachers must exercise great care not to magnify the number or importance of Jews in the Colonies. (At most there were then only two thousand Jews in America.) Likewise the role of Jews as merchants and businessmen should not be exaggerated. Though many were engaged in mercantile activities, substantial numbers were not. Haym Salomon should not be presented as the only Jew who gave financial support to the Continental army. Other Jews and numerous Christians provided money which all too often was not repaid, and, obviously, thousands of others suffered economic loss during the war. Francis Salvador, the sole Jewish delegate to any Colonial assembly or congress, is important because his singularity points up the fact that Jews played only a marginal political role in early American history.

American Jewish history during the Revolutionary era is intimately entwined with the struggle for religious equality. The Revolution meant an end to theocracy in America, the secularization and democratization of political authority, the transformation (enfranchisement) of subjects into citizens, the separation of church and state and the consequent transformation of the churches into voluntary associations, the abolition of civic distinctions among citizens based on religious affiliation, the abolition of religious tests as a qualification for holding political office, and the protection of the religious liberty for all citizens. George Washington's letter to the Newport Jewish community in 1790 suggests some of these themes, and the principles were enunciated in the Virginia Law to Establish Religious Freedom, the Northwest Ordinace, the Constitution of the United States, and the Bill of

Rights. The electoral principle is mandated in Article I of the Constitution (Congress) and in Article II (the President); Article VI forbids religious tests as a qualification for public office; and Article I of the Bill of Rights mandates the separation of church and state and protects religious liberty.

Students may reasonably ask, "If the Constitution is the supreme law of the land, why then was it not binding on the states?" The series of Constitutional decisions cited and the numerous incidents dealt with in this chapter help explain this and also shed light on the nature of the Fourteenth Amendment freedoms, as well. The discrepancy between the elemental changes wrought by the Revolution and actual practice of religious equality in the eighteenth century was substantial. In some states, statutory restrictions lingered well into the nineteenth century. The remainder of Chapter 4 details the closing of that gap in terms of the Jewish experience, which directly or indirectly benefited other minority groups and helped place America far ahead of Europe in guaranteeing social and political rights for all its citizens.

DISCUSSION QUESTIONS AND STUDENT ACTIVITIES

1. Write a biographical sketch about Lieutenant-Colonel David Salisbury Franks, an aid to Benedict Arnold on his retreat from Canada. Be sure to include the proceedings of the court of inquiry before which he sought to clear himself of possible implication in Arnold's treason.
2. Write an imaginary letter from David Franks, the famous Jewish Tory, to his relative, Lieutenant-Colonel Isaac Franks, justifying his support for George III. What reasons might he offer over and above those of a non-Jewish Tory? How might Isaac Franks have answered him?
3. Write an essay on the significance in American history of Francis Salvador, the sole Jewish delegate to any representative congress or assembly in Colonial America.
4. Compare George Washington's interpretation of the word "toleration" in his letter to the Newport Congre-

gation, to that of Thomas Paine in *The Rights of Man,* in which he wrote, "Toleration is not the opposite of intoleration, but it is the counterfeit of it. Both are despotisms." (See *The Complete Writings of Thomas Paine,* edited by Philip J. Foner, Citadel Press, New York, 1969, Vol. 1, p. 291, or any collection of Paine's writings.)

5. Conduct a debate on the proposition that no country should have an established church. For background read the Virginia Statute to Establish Religious Freedom, the Virginia Declaration of Rights, or the writings of James Madison, especially his "Memorial and Remonstrance against Religious Assessments" of 1784. Also consult the writings of Jefferson and some of the Enlightenment philosophers on this topic.
6. Prepare a chart indicating when each of the thirteen original colonies formally disestablished the Church. What pattern is discernible? Which was the last to do so and why?
7. Have students dramatize Jacob Henry's fight for equality in North Carolina. The highlight should be his speech in the North Carolina House of Commons in December, 1809. The full text with explanation will be found in *A Documentary History of the Jews in the United States,* by Morris U. Schappes, pp. 122-25 (listed in Basic Bibliography).
8. Write a series of newspaper articles detailing the progress of the "Maryland Jew Bill" during the period 1818 through 1826. Be sure to emphasize the role of Thomas Kennedy who was prominent in passage of the bill.
9. Write a brief biography of Uriah Phillips Levy. Be sure to stress his struggle against anti-Semitism, his role in ending corporal punishment in the United States Navy, and his efforts to restore Jefferson's home, Monticello. A good starting point will be either of the biographies of Levy listed in the bibliography of this chapter, or *A Jewish Tourist's Guide to the U.S.,* by Bernard Postal and Lionel Koppman, (listed in Basic Bibliography). See the entry for Charlottesville, Virginia, pp. 625-29.

10. Make a chart listing the following landmarks in the evolution of religious liberty in the United States:

    Article VI of the Constitution
    The First Amendment to the Constitution
    The Fourteenth Amendment to the Constitution
    The Northwest Ordinance
    The Virginia Law to Establish Religious Freedom

    The following Supreme Court decisions:

    Barron v. *Baltimore* (1833)
    Watson v. *Jones* (1872)
    The *Slaughterhouse* Cases (1873)
    Reynolds v. *United States* (1878)
    Meyer v. *Nebraska* (1923)
    Cantrell v. *Connecticut* (1940)

    Next to each indicate its contribution to religious liberty in the United States. Indicate which was most important. Explain. Some students might write briefs of the majority and minority opinion in each of the court decisions.
11. In what way was the decision in the case of *Barron* v. *Baltimore* (1833) an exception to most of the decisions rendered by the Supreme Court under Chief Justice John Marshall?
12. Does religious discrimination still exist in this country? Consider the following: Has there yet been a Jewish president of the United States or a Jewish governor in your state? Do Sunday work laws in some states discriminate against Jews or other religious minorities? Are Christmas trees in public schools constitutional? Do they offend Jews? Write a "position paper" on any or all of these topics.
13. Refer to any of the filmstrips listed in the bibliography to this chapter. Find an appropriate frame with several characters in it and have students "bring the scene to life" in a role play. Assign roles, create the scenario by reviewing what must have happened just before the picture "froze" the action. Let students assume their posi-

tions and improvise what comes next. Have several sets of students do the same exercise and see what different improvisations emerge.

BIBLIOGRAPHY

Abrahams, Robert D., *The Commodore: The Adventurous Life of Uriah P. Levy* (Jewish Publication Society, Philadelphia, 1954). The story of the famous Jewish naval hero who served in the War of 1812 and led the crusade against flogging in the United States Navy. An interesting and exciting biographical novel. Recommended for junior high students.

Fast, Howard M., *Haym Salomon: Son of Liberty* (Messner, New York, 1941). An interesting biographical novel of Haym Salomon. The style is simple; the book is suitable for high school and capable junior high school students.

Fitzpatrick, Donovan, and Saphire, Saul, *Navy Maverick: Uriah Phillips Levy* (Doubleday, New York, 1963). An exciting biography of Uriah Phillips Levy, his stormy naval career and personal struggle against anti-Semitism. The story emphasizes Levy's role in the passage of anti-flogging legislation in the United States Navy and his ownership of Jefferson's home at Monticello. Highly recommended for all students and teachers.

Friedman, Lee M., *Jewish Pioneers and Patriots* (Jewish Publications Society, Philadelphia, 1955). Chapter 1 is very good on Washington and the Jews. Chapter 2 concerns Jefferson and religious liberty. The book is well-written. Recommended for teachers and capable high school students.

Friedman, Lee M., *Pilgrims in a New Land* (Jewish Publication Society, Philadelphia, 1948). Chapters 1 through 6 are particularly relevant here. They include a number of important topics and biographical material which will be useful for student reports. Recommended for teachers and high school students.

Handlin, Oscar and Mary, "Acquisition of Political and Social Rights by the Jews in the United States," in *American Jewish Year Book,* Vol. 56, pp. 45-98, (Jewish Publication Society, Philadelphia, 1955). This is, perhaps, the best article available on the topic. Begins with the European background and carries the story down to 1954. Discusses the development of political, economic and social forces, and their embodiment in legislation which won for Jews a position of civic equality in America. An important essay which synthesizes much material. The authors frequently cite legal decisions, which is rare among writers on this topic. The article is a "must" for teachers who are interested in pursuing the subject and is suitable for capable high school students.

Huhner, Leon, *Jews in America After the American Revolution* (Gertz Bros., New York, 1959). Contains three essays. Of particular interest is the first, "The Struggle for Religious Liberty in North Carolina with Special Reference to the Jews," which provides good material on the struggle of Jacob Henry to retain his seat in the North Carolina legislature, including the text of Henry's speech. Recommended for teachers and better than average high school students. Excellent for research projects.

Konvitz, Milton R., *Fundamental Liberties of a Free People* (Cornell University Press, Ithaca, New York, 1957). Part I (chapters 1-13) is particularly concerned with religious freedom and church-state issues. Chapter 4 is especially good on Virginia's role in the struggle for religious freedom. Chapters 5 and 6 are excellent on the First and Fourteenth Amendments. Recommended for teachers and high school students.

Learsi, Rufus, *The Jews in America: A History* (Ktav Publishing House, Inc., New York, 1972). Chapter 3 deals with the Revolution and the struggle to secure equal rights in the various states. On page 48 there is a detailed, though incomplete explanation of why the Constitution failed to achieve this. Chapter 4 gives an account of the role of certain Jews during the War of 1812. Recommended for teachers and capable high school students.

Levinger, Lee J., *A History of the Jews in the United States* (Union of American Hebrew Congregations, New York, 1961). Chapter 8 of this high school text deals with Jews in the American Revolution and chapter 9 with Jews and religious freedom. Coverage is detailed but suitable for teachers and average high school students.

Marcus, Jacob R., *The Colonial American Jews, 1492-1776* (Wayne State University Press, Detroit, 1970). Chapters 16 through 25 are detailed but excellent on the legal and political status of Jews in British North America. Several chapters in volume 3 are particularly pertinent: Chapter 66, "Why Gentiles Accepted Jews," chapter 67, "Why Jews Accepted America," and chapters 72 through 76 which deal with Jews and the American Revolution. This is a gold mine of information for research. Recommended for teachers and advanced high school students.

St. John, Robert, *Jews, Justice and Judaism* (Doubleday, New York, 1969). Chapter 6 of this popular history is about the Revolution. It is especially strong on Haym Salomon, Jews in the Revolution, and the struggle for equal rights. Judah Touro and Uriah Phillips Levy are some of the figures discussed in Chapter 11. This material is suitable for teachers and average high school students.

AUDIO-VISUAL MATERIALS

Haym Salomon—Financier of the Revolution, a filmstrip produced by Eye Gate House, Inc., 1953. 30 frames, color, with text, part of the *Leaders of America Series.* Distributed by Filmstrip House, 432 Park Ave. South, New York, N. Y. 10016. This filmstrip tells of the life of Haym Salomon, his patriotism and financial support of the American Revolution, which is overemphasized. The artwork is good, but the story in general is sketchy. Recommended primarily for the junior high level.

Judah Touro—Friend of Man, a filmstrip produced by Victor Kayfetz Productions, Inc., 1953. 36 frames, color, includes 2 copies of teacher's guide. Distributed by the Commission on Jewish Education, Union of American Hebrew Congregations, 838 Fifth Ave., New York, N. Y. 10021. An accompanying 12-inch LP recording of the narration is also available. This is a prize-winning filmstrip depicting the life and work of Judah Touro, American Jewish patriot and philanthropist. It also emphasizes the growth of the American Jewish community. The artwork is good and the script is excellent. Suitable for junior and senior high school audiences.

The Pugnacious Sailing Master, a film produced by the Jewish Theological Seminary of America, 1954. 30 minutes, black and white. Distributed by the National Academy for Adult Jewish Studies of the United Synagogue of America, 218 E. 70th Street, New York, N. Y. 10021. This is an excellent instructional film telling the story of Uriah Phillips Levy, the highest ranking Jewish naval officer of his time. The film vividly depicts Levy's role in abolishing corporal punishment in the Navy as well as his crusade against anti-Semitism. Most suitable for junior high school students but could be used with high school groups, as well.

The Story of Haym Salomon, a filmstrip produced by the American Jewish Archives, 1952. 31 frames, color, includes text. Distributed by the Commission on Jewish Education, Union of American Hebrew Congregations, 838 Fifth Ave., New York, N. Y. 10021. This life of Haym Salomon begins in his native Poland and extends through his struggle for religious equality for Jews in Pennsylvania. The story is sketchy; it tries to cover too much ground, but nonetheless is useful. Recommended for both junior and senior high school audiences.

American Reform Judaism began in liberal Charleston, South Carolina when, in 1824, members of Charleston's Congregation Beth Elohim ("House of God") formed their own congregation.

CHAPTER III

BUILDING A NATIONAL IDENTITY

*

IMPORTANT EVENTS

1812 Napoleonic reforms end disabilities of German Jews.
1815 The Congress of Vienna nullifies rights of German Jews, leading to large-scale migration to America.
1848 Jewish political refugees join emigration from Germany.
1885 The Pittsburgh Platform is enunciated by Reform Jews, stating their principles and beliefs.

German Jewish Immigration

The second wave of Jewish immigration to the United States came from Germany. Jews had lived there since the beginning of the Christian era, when Roman legions brought Jewish slaves into the Rhine Valley from Palestine. Jews, however, were of little significance in Europe until the eighth century when Charlemagne invited their participation in finance and commerce and encouraged a large Jewish migration from Islamic Europe. Northern France and the Rhine Valley became the center of Jewish life within Christendom. A distinct trans-Alpine or German Jewry developed and prospered in this region as opposed to Spanish Jewry in the Mediterranean countries. One of the distinct characteristics of Jews in medieval and modern Europe was their persistent vulnerability to outbreaks of mass hysteria among the surrounding gentile population. Another was the fact that the Jewish minority was frequently confined to ghettos. Cut off from the Christian world, Jews developed a unique life style based on study of the Bible and the Talmud. It remained for the eighteenth century Enlightenment to bring about any substantial change in the pattern of Jewish life, both internally and in its relationship to the non-Jewish world.

Moses Mendelssohn, 1729-1786, an important figure in the Enlightenment, became the central figure in introducing secular culture to eighteenth-century European Jewry. As a result Jews became critics of their own Talmudic, rabbinically oriented way of life. Mendelssohn emphasized Judaism as a system of ethics. His greatest achievement was the translation of the Hebrew Bible into German, which provided Jews with a stepping stone to German culture. He encouraged German in place of Yiddish, the language of eastern European Jews. Yiddish is a Germanic language, a combination of Russian, German, Polish, Hebrew and other languages, written in the Hebrew alphabet. His work helped tear down political and social structures which set Jews apart from gentiles. Jews were encouraged to extend their intellectual and cultural horizons beyond the ghetto to the secular world.

Mendelssohn's efforts coincided with liberal reforms brought to Germany and other nations in Europe by Napoleon. Jewish political disabilities were swept away. By 1812 even restrictive Prussia had passed a major reform decree granting full equality and citizenship to Jews. Liberated from the mental and political ghettos of generations, Jews contributed to the astonishing cultural and intellectual life of Germany.

But with the defeat of Napoleon, their political emancipation came to an end. With few exceptions, the Congress of Vienna sought a return to the pre-revolutionary order in Europe which meant re-adoption of former attitudes toward Jews and nullification of rights they had gained. Anti-Jewish pamphlets and articles appeared in Germany and it became clear that Jews were again to be treated as inferiors.

Jews responded by either joining the liberal opposition to the reactionary social and political policies adopted by the governments that had recovered their powers after the defeat of Napoleon, or by departing for America. The exodus was not limited to Jews only. "Emigration fever" was everywhere. Poverty characterized an exhausted and backward

Germany. There was no central government, only a multiplicity of small states, each attempting to enforce its own petty autocracy and erase the liberal gains that had been achieved under Napoleon. With the sea routes open and safe again after the war, emigration began. By 1880, about 5,000,000 German immigrants had reached the United States. About 200,000 of them were Jews.

In some cases whole villages of German Jews departed *en masse,* leaving behind only empty houses and a deserted synagogue. They came not only from Germany, but from Austria, Hungary, Bohemia, and Rumania as well. The majority came from villages, but some left major cities like Berlin, Vienna, and Budapest. More German Jews came from Bavaria, where anti-Jewish laws were most severe, than from the other German states. Jews were heavily taxed; they were denied citizenship; they suffered under special regulations, controlling where they lived, where they worked, and where they travelled. Even the number of Jewish marriages was restricted. An inordinate number of Jewish immigrants, therefore, were young and single. When anti-Jewish restrictions were again dropped about the middle of the nineteenth century, the exodus of Jews slowed drastically.

Before 1848 the poorest, least educated Germans came to America. With the failure of the Revolution of 1848, a more liberal, intellectual refugee arrived. The best known of these "Forty-Eighters," as they were called, was the reformer Carl Schurz, a non-Jew. But the movement included many educated Jews, as well. Abraham Jacobi is a good example. He took part in the Revolution of 1848. He was arrested in 1849 and jailed for two years before escaping to America, where he was a prominent pediatrician. After 1850 the less educated immigrants again predominated. Most sought better economic or social conditions. A good example was Mayer Lehman, father of Justice Irving Lehman and Senator Herbert H. Lehman. He came when his brothers, who were already in the United States, were successful enough to pay his ocean passage.

By 1840 there were about 15,000 Jews in the United States. By 1850 there were 50,000, and by 1860 there were 150,000. By 1880 their numbers had swelled to 250,000. Most were of German origin. But Jews were still only one-half of one percent of the total population, despite the dramatic increase in their numbers since Revolutionary times, when the Jewish population had amounted to only 2,000. The German Jews had a far more lasting influence on Jewish life in America than did the Spanish Jews who had preceded them. They preferred to follow their own rituals and customs rather than to affiliate with the existing Spanish congregations, whose liturgy differed slightly from their own. Consequently, the nineteenth century witnessed a proliferation of congregations and new synagogues. In 1850 there were only thirty-seven congregations in the United States. In 1860 there were seventy-seven. By 1870 there were one hundred eight-nine.

Reform Judaism.

In these congregations a new trend was soon discernible. German Jews wanted to be Americanized rapidly. Demands were soon heard for shorter religious services, the use of English rather than Hebrew as the language of prayer, modification of the dietary laws, and elimination of many traditional restrictions which seemed pointless in America, where Jews mingled easily with Christians. Actually their demands were a manifestation of the Reform movement which had begun in Germany. Moses Mendelssohn had shaped its first outlines. The Reform movement among American Jews was an extension of the German Reform philosophy. It was an attempt by Jews to do away with the restrictions of the past—to accommodate themselves to their environment. Many felt it was a question of Judaism adapting quickly or dying. Traditionalists, on the other hand, were infuriated, maintaining that men could not so lightly change the ritual of hundreds of years. They considered Jewish law sacred; man was not to change what God had ordained.

American Reform Judaism began in liberal Charleston,

The ghetto in Frankfurt.

Isaac Mayer Wise (1818-1900), American Reform rabbi, founder of the Union of American Hebrew Congregations, the Hebrew Union College, and the Central Conference of American Rabbis.

South Carolina. In 1824 members of Charleston's Congregation *Beth Elohim* ("House of God") petitioned the trustees for reforms in the religious service. When their demands were refused they broke away and formed their own congregation. Thomas Jefferson took note of their efforts, commenting, "Nothing is wiser than that our institutions should keep pace with the advance of time and be improved with the improvement of the human mind." The Reform movement spread swiftly along the eastern seaboard and into the Ohio and Mississippi valleys.

Any discussion of Reform Judaism must stress the role of Isaac Mayer Wise. Born in Bohemia, he emigrated to America in 1846 where he became the rabbi of a small traditional congregation in Albany, New York, and gradually began introducing reforms in ritual. He soon produced a modified liturgy which introduced the use of English as its basic language. Wise dedicated his life to propagating Reform Judaism. He addressed congregations, founded newspapers, and wrote extensively, all with the aim of converting his fellow Jews to the new movement. By 1850 he had achieved national prominence. In 1854 he accepted a rabbinical post in Cincinnati, at that time one of the largest Jewish communities in the country and the center of the Reform movement.

In Philadelphia, Isaac Leeser, another German-Jewish immigrant, led the traditional congregation in that city. An outspoken opponent of innovation in Jewish worship, he became the leader of traditional, or Orthodox, Judaism in America. In 1843 Leeser founded the *Occident,* a monthly magazine devoted to Jewish affairs, and used it to denounce Wise's new liturgy. For twenty-five years Leeser, in the East, defended the traditionalists, generally of Spanish origin, while Wise, in the Midwest, led the Reformers, generally of German background.

Despite Leeser's efforts, by 1870 Reform Judaism had become an established part of Jewish life in America. Year by year additional Reform congregations were organized and a seminary for the training of Reform rabbis was founded in

1875. In 1885 nineteen Reform rabbis met in Pittsburgh under the chairmanship of Rabbi Wise. They adopted a manifesto of the principles and beliefs of Reform Judaism. It embraced the moral teachings of Judaism but rejected traditional practices "not adapted to the views and habits of modern civilization." With some significant modifications, it is still accepted by Reform Jews.

The German Jewish Community

A well-marked feature of American life, emphasized by De Tocqueville in *Democracy in America,* is the multitude and variety of voluntary organizations which have sprung up to fill social and political needs. The tradition of communal self-help and voluntarism in America has always been strong, and accounts in part, no doubt, for the relative tardiness of, and resistance to, the coming of the welfare state in this country. The Jewish community epitomized the zeal with which groups in America have founded private, voluntary organizations, and the German Jewish immigrants largely inaugurated this development within the American Jewish community. They took Jewish philanthropic and social life out of the synagogue and centered it in a number of other institutions.

With the rising tide of immigration from Europe, Jewish charity was severely strained. Many of the immigrants were destitute. They often arrived with little more than the clothes on their backs. In the smaller communities there was often one central, all-purpose charitable organization, usually called "The Hebrew Benevolent Society." In the larger cities a number of societies developed to meet charitable and social needs. Separate societies usually formed for specific kinds of help: care of orphans, assistance to the poor, and visiting the sick. Burial societies provided consecrated ground for the indigent dead and free loan societies advanced money without interest. There were even such highly specialized charities as those which provided unleavened bread (*matzah*) for the Passover holiday.

By 1860 five national fraternal orders had appeared, the

best known being B'nai B'rith (Sons of the Covenant). B'nai B'rith was founded in New York in 1843 by twelve newly arrived German Jewish immigrants who decided to form a society which would offer a program of culture, philanthropy, and mutual aid. By 1860 it had more than fifty lodges. The Anti-Defamation League of B'nai B'rith, founded in 1913, protects Jews and other minorities from attack or slander.

Among the social and literary societies which sprang up during this period, the Young Men's Hebrew Association (YMHA) was the best known. The Hebrew "Y" still helps meet the cultural and social needs of the Jewish community.

Jewish hospitals were established in Cincinnati in 1850 and in New York in 1856 to meet the religious and dietary needs of Jewish patients. At first they limited themselves to the care of Jews. Christians were admitted only in case of emergency. But during the Civil War, so many non-Jewish patients were treated that the hospitals became non-sectarian institutions. Jewish-supported hospitals in other cities also became nonsectarian and this has remained the norm to the present day.

Just as the Jewish community founded its own philanthropic institutions instead of relying exclusively on those of the surrounding community, so too it founded its own schools, though at a later date Jews abandoned this effort, for the most part, and became strong supporters of the public school system. Though the movement in the North for all-day public schools was growing in the mid-1800's, most congregations still supported parochial schools which taught both Jewish and secular subjects. Some upheld high standards, but most offered an inadequate religious education in the absence of qualified teachers and suitable textbooks. Some of the older, more established congregations sponsored Sunday schools, but like the parochial schools, they were strong on the secular and weak on the religious curriculum. The decade of the 1860's saw the decline of Jewish day schools as more and more Jewish students attended public schools during the day and Sunday schools or late-

Michael Reese Hospital in Chicago, Illinois, named after the Jewish philanthropist (1817-1878). It was built by the United Hebrew Charities and is still in existence.

afternoon religious schools for their Jewish education.

Although there were many local private voluntary agencies that sprang up in the course of the ninteenth century to meet a variety of needs, there was no one organization that could claim to represent or speak for American Jews. There were occasions when a leader able to speak in the name of American Jewry as a whole might have been helpful. In 1840 a monk and his servant disappeared in Damascus. Thirteen Jews there were arrested and charged with kidnapping. Though the presidents of the Board of Deputies of British Jews and the *Alliance Israelite Universelle,* representing French Jewry, successfully interceded with the Turkish governor, American Jews, lacking a national spokesman, could do no more than hold protest meetings. When some Swiss cantons restricted the travel of American Jews, the American Jewish community was equally impotent. Much the same was true in 1879, when a naturalized American Jew returned to Russia and was denied the right to buy land. The Russian government maintained that a Russian Jew who had migrated to America, even though naturalized, remained a Russian subject, bound by the prevailing restriction against land ownership which applied to all Russian Jews. (This policy clashed with the American view, for Congress in 1868 had explicitly declared voluntary expatriation "a natural and inherent right of all people.")

These and other incidents led to periodic attempts to establish a national organization of American Jews. Neither in the nineteenth century nor subsequently were these efforts successful. There were many reasons for this. Jews in America, like other religious groups, were members of purely voluntary associations in the eyes of the state. Jewishness did not have legal status in the United States as it often did in Europe. It conferred neither privileges nor disabilities which Jews had to organize either to claim or to fight. There was no hierarchy in Judaism. Then as now, congregations were autonomous. American Jewry was too diverse, the country too large, the numerous local philanthropies too jealous of their prerogatives to permit the emergence of any one national organization which could unify all or even most American Jews. There are, however, a number of national organizations such as B'nai B'rith, the Anti-Defamation League, the American Jewish Committee, and the American Jewish Congress, which have a wide following. But before 1860 they were yet to assume that role.

TO THE TEACHER:

Immigration and cultural pluralism are continued in this chapter. The concept of America as a land of opportunity is introduced with the active participation of German Jews in the settlement of the Ohio and Mississippi valleys before the Civil War. Their migration also provides a rich source of material on the process of acculturation and assimilation in American society. The struggle between nineteenth-century Reform Judaism and the more traditional elements which opposed it provides a helpful analogy for teaching general political concepts involving the liberal, moderate, and conservative positions. The phenomenal rise of Reform Judaism which encouraged American Jews to emulate their Christian neighbors and the failure of the Jewish day schools to take root in the nineteenth century foreshadowed the melting-pot theory. It provides a striking contrast to the current emphasis on ethnic and cultural diversity, as well as to the self-segregating orthodoxy which flourished in the less hospitable environments of Europe.

Nineteenth-century American-Jewish philanthropy reflects on the conflict between private and public sources of welfare in this country. The relatively late arrival of the welfare state in America can be explained, in some measure, by the strong emphasis on voluntarism and community self-help in which these early German-Jewish communities, among others, excelled.

The absence of any representative national Jewish organization in the nineteenth century refutes the idea of uniformity in the Jewish community even then. No single organization could represent "Jewish opinion," for even at this early date there was no typical American Jew. Nineteenth-century diplomatic clashes with Switzerland and Russia concerning equal rights for American Jews revealed the absence of such a representative national body. The Russian view of the inviolability of citizenship as contrasted to the American defense of voluntary expatriation is an issue containing the elements of an excellent classroom debate.

DISCUSSION QUESTIONS AND STUDENT ACTIVITIES

1. Compare the "emancipation" of the Jews in Germany to the emancipation of the slaves in America and the serfs in Russia. What similarities and differences are there?
2. What metaphor would be helpful in explaining the position of Germany's Jews after the Congress of Vienna? Keep in mind that they had been emancipated and suddenly found their freedom taken away. Try these for a start: "Pulling the rug from under," "Indian-giver," "a mirage in the desert." How many such analogies can you list? Next to each explain how it resembles the plight of the Jews in Germany and how it differs. Put an asterisk next to your best one.
3. Compare the situation of the German Jews following the Congress of Vienna in 1815, with that of Russian Jews today. What were the significant similarities and differences?
4. Prepare a comparative study of the German-Jewish immigration of the nineteenth century and that of another ethnic group. What were the similarities and differences between the two? What principles can you formulate about the causes of migration?
5. In some ways migration is like magnetism. Attracting forces pull settlers to the new country, repelling forces drive them from the old. Prepare a list of all the forces which influenced the German Jews to come to America in the mid-nineteenth century. Ask your parents or grandparents why and from where your ancestors came to America. Prepare a similar list. Compare differences and similarities.

6. Organize committees to visit Reform, Conservative, and Orthodox synagogues. Attend a service, if possible. In what ways is it similar to a church? In what ways is it different? Each committee should report its findings to the class. Which is most appealing to you?
7. Compare the efforts of Reform Judaism to modernize and Americanize its observance and rituals with modernization efforts of another religious group in the United States, perhaps your own religion if you are not Jewish.
8. From where do the basic Jewish concepts of charity derive? How do they help explain the numerous charitable institutions developed by the German Jews in America in the nineteenth century? Read the Bible, Deuteronomy 15:7-11, for a start. Also refer to Maimonides' "Eight Degrees of Charity," in the *Mishneh Torah*. (See Maimonides, *Mishneh Torah*, edited by Phillip Birnbaum, Hebrew Publishing Co., New York, 1967, pp. 158-59, or ask your librarian for help. Also try the library of a synagogue.) A good discussion of the Jewish concept of charity will be found in *A Book of Jewish Concepts* by Philip Birnbaum, Hebrew Publishing Co., New York, 1964, pp. 520-23, and in *Jews, Justice and Judaism,* by Robert St. John, pp. 250-51, (listed in the bibliography of this chapter).
9. Prepare a list of as many Jewish organizations as you can identify in your city. Compare at least one to a similar organization sponsored by another religious or ethnic group. A book you might refer to is *American Jewish Yearbook* (listed in Basic Bibliography). The list of Jewish organizations in the appendix of this book may also be helpful.
10. Prepare a research report on the reaction of American Jews to any of the following international problems in the nineteenth century. What did their reactions reveal about national unity, or the lack of it, among American Jews in the nineteenth century?
    1. The Damascus Incident, 1840.

2. Nineteenth Century U.S.—Swiss relations concerning American Jews.
3. Nineteenth century U.S.—Russian relations concerning American Jews.

A helpful source is *With Firmness in the Right* by Cyrus Adler and Aaron Margalith (listed in the bibliography of this chapter).

BIBLIOGRAPHY

Adler, Cyrus, and Margalith, Aaron M., *With Firmness in the Right: American Diplomatic Action Affecting Jews, 1840-1945* (American Jewish Committee, New York, 1946). A major study of U.S. diplomacy relating to Jews. Cyrus Adler was a leading figure in the Jewish community until his death in 1940. Chapter 1 deals with the Damascus affair; Chapter 7 with United States-Russian relations, focusing on the rights of American Jews in Russia; and chapter 10 concerns discrimination against American Jews in Switzerland. Recommended for teachers and above-average high school students.

Cohon, Samuel S., "Reform Judaism in America," in *Jewish Life in America* edited by Theodore Friedman and Robert Gordis (Horizon Press, New York, 1955), pp. 75-108. This article is a good account of the Reform movement in the history of American Judaism. Suitable for teachers and high school students.

Gay, Ruth, *Jews in America* (Basic Books, New York, 1965). Chapter 2, "Wayfaring Strangers," deals with the German-Jewish migration of the nineteenth century. Contains a good discussion of the development of Reform Judaism in America. Suitable for teachers and junior and senior high school students.

Glazer, Nathan, *American Judaism* (University of Chicago Press, Second Edition, Chicago, 1972, also in paperback). Chapter 3 is an interesting survey of the German-Jewish immigration of the nineteenth century and the development of Reform Judaism in America. The full text of the Pittsburgh Platform is included in Appendix A. Recommended for teachers and superior high school students.

Handlin, Oscar, *Adventure in Freedom: Three Hundred Years of Jewish Life in America* (McGraw-Hill, New York, 1954). Chapter 3 provides good coverage of the European background to the German-Jewish migration and the place of the German Jews in an expanding American society. Chapter 4 sheds light on their cultural, religious, and organizational life. Recommended for teachers and capable high school students.

Hirshler, Eric E. (ed.), *Jews from Germany in the United States* (Farrar, Straus and Cudahy, New York, 1955). Essays dealing with Jews from Germany. The major essay by Dr. Hirshler, bearing the same title as the book, will be most useful. Also includes units on the "Russian" immigration and the more recent German immigration during the Hitler era. Much of the material it contains is valuable. Recommended for teachers and capable high school students.

Korn, Bertram W., *Eventful Years and Experiences: Studies in Nineteenth Century American Jewish History* (The American Jewish Archives, Cincinnati, 1954). Essays on nineteenth century topics. The first two deal with Jewish "Forty-Eighters" in America and American Jewish life in 1849. Dr. Korn emphasizes the growing trend toward national Jewish organization. For teachers and capable high school students doing research.

Learsi, Rufus, *The Jews in America: A History* (Ktav, New York, 1972). Chapter 8, "Religious Divisions," traces the development of Reform Judaism and the Wise-Leeser feud. For teachers and capable high school students.

Levinger, Lee J., *A History of the Jews in the United States* (Union of American Hebrew Congregations, New York, 1961). Chapter 12 deals with the German-Jewish immigration of the mid-nineteenth century. Chapters 14 and 15 are concerned with the growth and development of Reform Judaism. Chapter 16 is about German-Jewish communal life. Recommended for teachers and junior and senior high school students.

Pessin, Deborah, *History of the Jews in America* (United Synagogue of America, New York, 1957). Unit III, Chapter 2 emphasizes Jewish education, voluntarism, and the religious development of the German-Jews. Chapter 5 deals with the development of Orthodox, Conservative, and Reform Judaism. Includes good material on the Wise-Leeser feud. Suitable primarily for junior high school readers.

St. John, Robert, *Jews, Justice and Judaism* (Doubleday, New York, 1969). Chapter 8 discusses the development of Reform Judaism. Chapter 10 is a good presentation of the Wise-Leeser controversy and Chapter 19 deals with Jewish philanthropy. Recommended for teachers and high school students.

AUDIO-VISUAL MATERIALS

David Einhorn: The Father of the Union Prayer Book, a filmstrip produced by Samuel Grand, 1960, 41 frames, color. Sponsored and distributed by the Commission on Jewish Education, Union of American Hebrew Congregations, 838 Fifth Ave., New York, N. Y. 10021. This production portrays the life of Rabbi David Einhorn, an abolitionist and leader of Reform Judaism in America. The Union Prayer Book is the prayer book of Reform Judaism. The filmstrip is suitable for coordination with this chapter and with lessons on the Civil War (chapter 7). Recommended for high school audiences.

Isaac Mayer Wise: Master Builder of American Judaism, a filmstrip produced and distributed by the Commission on Jewish Education, Union of American Hebrew Congregations, 838 Fifth Ave., New York, N. Y. 10021, 1953. 36 frames, color, includes 2 copies of teacher's guide. This well-researched filmstrip tells of Isaac Mayer Wise's role in establishing Reform Judaism in the United States. The title is misleading. It should have been "Master Builder of Reform Judaism in America." Recommended for high school audiences. The script is excellent but some of the abstract phrases and concepts dealt with might be confusing for junior high students.

Jewish Life in the Middle Ages, a filmstrip in 2 parts, produced and distributed by the Audio-Visual Department, Bureau of Jewish Education, 590 N. Vermont Ave., Los Angeles, California 90004, 1961. 40 frames each, color. Part 1 "The Sad Centuries," describes the medieval world and reviews Jewish community life from its origins in Europe to the end of the eighteenth century. Part 2, "Life in The Ghetto," emphasizes the ghetto in Italy and Germany. Both will be useful for background to the German immigration. The script and artwork are good. Recommended for junior and senior high school audiences.

The King's Hunchback, a kinescope film of the NBC-TV Religious Hour Program, "Frontiers of Faith," produced by the Jewish Theological Seminary of America in cooperation with the National Broadcasting Company, 1953. 30 minutes, black and white. Distributed by the National Academy for Adult Jewish Studies in the United Synagogue of America, 218 E. 70th St., New York, N. Y. 10021. This is a highly recommended film, portraying episodes in the life of the German-Jewish philosopher, Moses Mendelssohn, and his relationship with Frederick the Great concerning religious freedom. Suitable for background to the German-Jewish migration to America. For junior and senior high school audiences.

Moses Mendelssohn: Pioneer In Modern Judaism, a filmstrip produced by Samuel Grand, 1958. 43 frames, color, with 12-inch LP recorded narration. Includes 2 copies of teacher's guide. Sponsored and distributed by the Commission on Jewish Education, Union of American Hebrew Congregations, 838 Fifth Ave., New York, N. Y. 10021. This filmstrip portrays the life of the great Jewish philosopher, highlighting his struggle to achieve civil equality for Jews in Germany and to introduce them to Western culture. Provides useful background on the German-Jewish immigration of the nineteenth century. An excellent piece of work, combining good artwork with an information-packed script. Suitable for high school audiences.

Julius Meyer (1851-1909) of Omaha, Nebraska, an Indian trader in the 1870's, with some of his Indian friends.

CHAPTER IV

WESTWARD EXPANSION

*

IMPORTANT EVENTS

1817	The first Jew settles in Cincinnati, Ohio, which by 1850 becomes a major center of Judaism in America.
1817-1860	Jews migrate westward.
1817-1860	Jewish peddlers epitomize the development of American capitalism.
1846-1848	Jews serve in the American armed forces during the Mexican War.
1849	Jews join the California Gold Rush—hold first High Holy Day services in San Francisco.

Midwestern Settlements

While some German immigrants remained in the East, many, Jews and non-Jews alike, were drawn to the wide open spaces and fertile lands of the Ohio and Mississippi Valleys. Some followed the frontier to the Pacific.

The majority of German Jews at first settled in the Midwest. Most settlers tended to purchase land or obtain it free as homesteaders. Jews, on the other hand, coming to America largely from small towns, with little experience or tradition in agriculture because they had been excluded from it in Europe, rarely became farmers. They usually settled in towns or cities. Many were attracted to peddling which required little capital. Others became tailors, brewers, watchmakers, carpenters, shoemakers, hunters, newspaper editors, politicians, doctors, lawyers, and craftsmen in a variety of different fields. They tended to disperse geographically, seeking business locations away from competition.

The first Jew reached Cincinnati in 1817. Others soon followed, and by 1824 Congregation *B'nai Israel* (Sons of Israel) was organized. Its history typifies that of most other Jewish congregations of this time. It gradually expanded, adding buildings and a school. By 1850 there were several other congregations and approximately 2,500 Jews in Cincinnati. Ten years later there were four times that number as Cincinnati assumed a leading role in American Jewish affairs. It was here that Max Lilienthal and Isaac Mayer Wise, both prominent rabbis, were to organize the Reform movement in American Judaism.

Jewish communities were established by the middle of the nineteenth century in Cleveland, Columbus, Dayton, Akron, Chicago, Louisville, Indianapolis, Milwaukee, Detroit, St. Louis, and in many smaller cities, as well.

The first generation of German Jews generally did not enter public life. Their children, however, either born or educated in the United States, did. Oscar Straus, at different times Theodore Roosevelt's Secretary of Commerce and Labor, was America's first Jewish cabinet member. Henry Morgenthau served as ambassador to Turkey and headed a presidential commission under Woodrow Wilson. Irving Lehman was a Justice of the New York State Court of Appeals, and his brother Herbert was Governor of New York and later United States Senator. All were sons of German-Jewish immigrants. Occasionally, the immigrants themselves achieved prominence. Adolph Kraus, a "Forty-Eighter," is a good example. He arrived from Bohemia in 1850 at the age of sixteen, poor and knowing little English. He became a leading lawyer and prominent figure in Chicago, as well as international president of B'nai B'rith. Michael Heilprin became one of the editors of Appleton's *New American Cyclopaedia* and foreign affairs writer for the old *Nation*. He later helped found Jewish agricultural colonies and became an ardent abolitionist. Solomon Kuhn went into banking and later merged his business with the Loeb Company to form Kuhn, Loeb and Company.

Jewish Peddlers

Many of the immigrants arriving during this period, Christians as well as Jews, lacked professional training or capital. They frequently turned to peddling, a livelihood requiring no formal training and little capital so that most were able to outfit a pack with a variety of household goods and trudge through the countryside selling their wares. They also brought news and gossip into areas reached by few other people. Their arrival at the farmhouse doorstep was often a bright spot in the dreary life of the pioneer housewife. Their lives were difficult in the lonely wilderness of America, cut off from family, friends, and for the Jewish peddlers the comfort of Jewish ritual and worship. For them the synagogue was a haven of warmth and friendship after weeks on the road.

From these humble beginnings, some peddlers managed to accumulate enough cash to buy a cart, then a horse and buggy, and finally a small store which in some cases later developed into large department stores. Some stores founded by Jewish peddlers are Altman's, Macy's, Bloomingdale's, Magnin's, Gimbel's, and Abraham and Strauss. The majority, however, remained small or medium-sized retailers. Yet, the history of German-Jewish peddling reflects at least one facet of the development of American enterprise. In the transition from itinerant peddler to prosperous retailer, there was at work a combination of opportunity, necessity, and hard work, to which the immigrants accommodated themselves. In this respect their experience paralleled that of untold other Americans who, by much the same process, helped build American industry in the nineteenth century.

The Frontier

Jews were among the earliest migrants to the Southwest and the Far West, and immediately became an integral part of the frontier environment. Sometimes it was a Jew who first settled a village or town. Jews helped build the city of Galveston, Texas, which had a Jewish mayor in the 1850's.

A Jewish-owned firm on State Street, Salt Lake City, Utah, in the 1870's.

The first ladies' clothing store of I. Magnin, who became a leading California retailer.

Some western towns, such as Mayer and Solomonsville, Arizona; Levy, New Mexico; Newman, California; Altman, Colorado; Altheimer, Arkansas; and Roseburg, Oregon, were named after Jews, and still bear witness to their early presence, as do Rose Canyon, California; Weiss Bluff, Texas; and Mount Davidson, Nevada. Jews became buffalo hunters, ranchers, distillers, ferrymen, newspaper editors, mayors, government agents, photographers, miners, explorers, fur traders, and more. They freely participated in the civic and cultural life of the frontier.

Solomon Nuñes Carvalho was an artist and photographer. He travelled with John Charles Frémont on his fifth expedition into the West. In his diary, Carvalho vividly describes deserts and prairies teeming with buffalo, deer, and antelope. Julius Meyer was a storekeeper in Omaha. He learned the languages of the Huron, Chippewa, and Pottawatomie Indians with whom he traded. Jacob Isaacson, a California merchant, went deep into the Santa Cruz Valley in Arizona to trade with the Indians. In New Mexico, a rabbi named Jim Harper earned extra money as a rider in a Wild West show. In Colorado, Otto Mears prospected for gold and helped build railroads, yet found time to study the Talmud. In Texas, Samuel Isaacs was among Stephen Austin's first settlers in 1821 and Moses Albert Levy was Surgeon General under Sam Houston. In Europe any one of these men might have been confined to a small town, or perhaps a ghetto. In America they were pioneers.

In Texas, Samuel Isaacs was among Stephen Austin's first settlers, in 1821. Several Jews fought under General Sam Houston. His surgeon-general, for example, was Moses Albert Levy. A few Jewish settlers in Texas achieved prominence in politics. One, Adolphus Sterne, served in the legislature of the Texas Republic and after annexation in 1845 represented Texas in the United States Congress.

Occasionally during the German-Jewish period, a Jew of Spanish background stands out. Henry Castro successfully promoted a colonization project for Sam Houston. From

A portrait of himself by Solomon Nuñes Carvalho (1815-1897), adventurous and talented Jewish artist, photographer and explorer, who crossed the Rocky Mountains with John Charles Frémont's expedition in 1854.

1843 to 1846, he was responsible for the settlement of about 5,000 Germans in the Republic of Texas. Castro County was named for him, as well as the little town of Castroville, west of San Antonio. During the Mexican War, fifty-six Jews served in the armed forces. Outstanding among them was an army surgeon, David Camden de Leon, of South Carolina, who was nicknamed "the fighting doctor" after he led a cavalry charge at the Battle of Chapultepec. De Leon later joined the Confederate army as Surgeon General and helped organize its medical service.

The Gold Rush

Like others, Jews joined the gold rush in California in 1849, and also like others, rarely struck it rich. They searched for gold during the day and often held prayers in the evening in a tent or under the open sky. On *Yom Kippur* (Day of Atonement) in 1849, forty Jewish pioneers held services in a room over a store in San Francisco. By 1850 two congregations had been organized in California. The first Jewish cemetery plot was purchased with $500 in gold dust, contributed by a Jewish prospector who had struck it rich.

An immigrant Jewish peddler named Levi Strauss unwittingly became famous and wealthy. One day in California he tried to sell some burlap to a miner who informed him that what he really needed was a good, strong pair of pants that would stand up to the rough treatment they received in the mines. Strauss and an immigrant Jewish tailor teamed up to make trousers of denim, the pockets reinforced with copper rivets to bear the weight of the miners' heavy tools and ingots. The first "Levis" were a huge success.

Two Jews, Solomon Heydenfeldt and Henry Lyons, became Associate Justices of the California Supreme Court, and a brother of Heydenfeldt was a member of the state legislature. In Wyoming, Meyer Guggenheim, a peddler from Pennsylvania, and his sons, founded huge mining and smelting enterprises. Their name is well known today to scholars and artists who have received fellowships from the John Simon

An advertisement for Levi Strauss and Co.'s copper-riveted clothing. Strauss, a German immigrant and prominent citizen of San Francisco, created a mercantile empire that still thrives.

Guggenheim Memorial Foundation, and to thousands of visitors each year to the Solomon R. Guggenheim Museum in New York City.

* * *

In the nineteenth century, as now, American Jews were not a uniform group. They were as diverse in occupation, ability, economic status, and geographical location as other Americans. Of those who moved West, few ever became rich or famous, but freed from old world prejudices and restraints they were able to participate actively in the settlement of the United States.

TO THE TEACHER:

This chapter relates the German-Jewish immigration to the settlement of the American West. Jews were present in the several advancing belts of settlement identified by Frederick Jackson Turner in his frontier thesis. They pursued a variety of occupations, but rarely became farmers. Their occupational and geographic diversity underscores the recurring themes of heterogeneity among Jews and of America as a land relatively free of Old World bigotry, where ability was the principal ingredient in a man's success. Jews often rose high in the fields they chose. This theme might be contrasted to current demands for ethnic, racial, and sexual quotas in employment and university enrollment. "To what extent," the teacher might ask his students, "is a society justified in encouraging a quota system instead of one based solely on merit?"

The history of German-Jewish peddling, as is clear from the text, provides an illustration of the nature of the American free enterprise system and suggests an analogy to the rise of industry, in general. The number of Jews in frontier America was relatively small, and, as was true of the Revolutionary period, should not be exaggerated. The presence of Jews, along with members of other minority groups, nonetheless, provides an index to the scope and variety of ethnic participation in settling the American West. Their inclusion in the curriculum would help correct some of the omissions of most American history texts.

DISCUSSION QUESTIONS AND STUDENT ACTIVITIES

1. Visit a synagogue in your city. Try to learn about its historical origins and some of the early personalities associated with it. Possible sources include published yearbook accounts of its history; archive materiai in its library; discussions with congregants; examination of cornerstones, wall plaques and inscriptions for important dates, names, and other information; interviews with the rabbi and members of the religious school faculty. Summarize your findings on a report.
2. On an outline map of the United States, indicate as many towns and places named after early Jewish pioneers or settlers as possible. A good source will be *A Jewish Tourist's Guide to the U.S.* by Bernard Postal and Lionel Kopman (listed in Basic Bibliography). Prepare a report on the history and significance of those closest to your home.
3. Write a letter to the public relations department of a large department store, such as Macy's, Gimbel's, Bloomingdale's, or the May stores. Ask for material on the early history of the store. Was it founded by one of the early German-Jewish peddlers? Prepare a report for the class.
4. You are a Jewish peddler in the Midwest. Write an account of your travels for one year. Be sure to include:
    a. places you visited
    b. things you sold
    c. places you lived
    d. people you met
    e. your feelings
    f. how you were received by individuals and by communities
    g. your financial gain (or loss)
5. Write an essay on the Jews and the settlement of the West. Relate the history of early Jewish peddlers and mer-

chants to Frederick Jackson Turner's "Frontier Thesis." How does their presence support (or refute) the idea of advancing belts of settlement?

6. Write to the public relations department of Levi Strauss and Co., 98 Battery Street, San Francisco, California, 94106, and ask for information on the history of the company and its founder, Levi Strauss. Write a report on your findings.
7. Compare O. E. Rolväag's *Giants in the Earth* with some aspect of Jewish western settlement.
8. Write a biographical report on any of the following Jews in American history:

Solomon Nuñes Carvalho	Adolph Kraus
Henry Castro	Solomon Kuhn
Louis Fleischner	Henry Lyons
Michael Heilprin	Henry Morgenthau
Solomon Heydenfeldt	Otto Mears
Abraham Jacobi	Oscar Straus

9. Conduct a discussion or assign essays on the topic, "What is so strange about a Jewish cowboy?" Refer to various Jews in the history of the American West. Be sure to include and explain stereotyping.

BIBLIOGRAPHY

Apsler, Alfred, *Western Pioneers* (Jewish Publication Society, Philadelphia, 1960), is the story of Louis Fleischner and the foundation of the first Jewish community in the Pacific Northwest. Fleischner and his younger brother followed the Oregon trail to the Far West, where he became an outstanding citizen. Recommended for junior high school students.

Carvalho, Solomon Nuñes, *Incidents of Travel and Adventure in the Far West* (Jewish Publication Society, Philadelphia, 1954). This text by Solomon Nuñes Carvalho is the only known detailed source for John Charles Frémont's fifth expedition to the Far West, since Fremont entered political life immediately afterwards and never wrote about it. It is also the only extended narrative of western American adventure in the mid-nineteenth century by a Jew. Suitable for teachers and capable high school students.

Friedman, Lee M., *Pilgrims in a New Land* (Jewish Publication Society, Philadelphia, 1948). Chapter 20 deals with the role of Jewish merchants in American history. It includes a discussion of German-Jewish peddlers in America. Recommended for teachers and high school students.

Gay, Ruth, *Jews in America* (Basic Books, New York, 1965). Chapter 3, "Wayfaring Strangers," contains a good discussion of Jewish peddlers in mid-nineteenth-century America. Suitable for teachers and junior and senior high school students.

Greenspan, Sophie, *Westward With Frémont, The Story of Solomon Carvalho* (Jewish Publication Society, Philadelphia, 1969). An excellent historical biography for young readers. It might be used in conjunction with Carvalho's own writing about his travels with Frémont (see above). Recommended for junior high school students.

Handlin, Oscar, *Adventure in Freedom: Three Hundred Years of Jewish Life in America* (McGraw-Hill, New York, 1954). Chapter 3, "The Problems of an Expanding Society," offers an interesting analysis of the economic role of Jews in the westward movement of the mid-nineteenth century. Chapter 5 also includes several pages about Jewish peddlers and Jewish mercantile interests. Suitable for teachers and high school students.

Ish Kishor, Sulamith, *American Promise, A History of the Jews in the New World* (Behrman House, New York, 1947). Chapter 9, "Wagons Break Trail," deals with Jews in the westward movement of America during the late eighteenth and early nineteenth centuries. Chapter 11 continues the story with the arrival of German-Jewish immigrants after 1816. Recommended for junior high school readers.

Learsi, Rufus, *The Jews in America: A History* (Ktav, New York, 1972). Chapter 5, "Across the Continent," deals with the German-Jewish immigration of the mid-nineteenth century. Learsi handles the material well. Emphasis is on midwestern settlements. For teachers and capable high school students.

Levinger, Elma Ehrlich, *Jewish Adventures in America* (Bloch Publishing Co., New York, 1954). Part II gives biographical sketches of numerous Jewish participants in the growth of America in the nineteenth century. Suitable for junior high school students.

Pessin, Deborah, *History of the Jews in America* (United Synagogue of America, New York, 1957). Unit III, Chapter 1, "Pioneers From the Germanic Lands" parallels this chapter. It gives a good account of Jewish peddlers. Chapter 3, "Trail-Blazers," contains some very colorful material on Jewish participation in the march westward. See also, "Yankee Notions," pp. 269-276 for a good sketch of peddling in the early nineteenth century. For students at the junior high school reading level.

St. John, Robert, *Jews, Justice and Judaism* (Doubleday, New York, 1969). Chapters 7 and 9 deal with the "Forty-Eighters," and with settlements in the Midwest and Farwest. Suitable for teachers and high school students.

Vorspan, Max, and Gartner, Lloyd P., *History of the Jews of Los Angeles* (Jewish Publication Society of America, Philadelphia, 1970). Chapter 1 is about the gold rush period. Chapters 2 and 3 cover the period 1860-1880. All give a useful description of Jews in the Far West. Ample detail makes this suitable for capable high school students doing research projects and for teachers.

Audio-Visual Note: Appropriate sections of the three comprehensive filmstrips listed under Basic Audio-Visual Materials in the Introduction to this book may be used in connection with this chapter. Unfortunately, good audio-visual materials which deal specifically with the role of Jews in the West do not exist.

Judah P. Benjamin (1811-1884), Confederate statesman. A senator from Louisiana, he became Attorney-General of the Confederacy, acting Secretary of War, and Secretary of State. He fled to England after the war.

CHAPTER V

CIVIL WAR AND RECONSTRUCTION

*

IMPORTANT EVENTS

1861 Rabbi Raphall discourses on the Biblical view of slavery.
1862 Rabbis are permitted to serve as military chaplains.
1862 General Grant issues General Order No. 11, expelling Jews, as a class, from the Department of the Tennessee.
1886 Jewish Theological Seminary is established, marking the arrival of the Conservative Jewish Movement in America.
1877 Joseph Seligman and family are excluded from fashionable resort hotel.

In April, 1861, 150,000 Jews lived in the United States. Most of them had recently emigrated from Germany. In normal times the immigrant assimilates slowly, relinquishing his old-world heritage little by little. The pressures of civil war denied the German Jew this luxury. In both North and South, Jewish immigrants absorbed the attitudes of their neighbors, shared with them the tragedy of war, and more keenly than ever accepted their responsibilities in their adopted country. The fervor with which most American Jews identified with one side or the other and the contribution they made during the Civil War suggests how completely they had entered into American life. Ten thousand Jews served in the Union and Confederate armies, most of them in the Union Army. Others raised money for the war effort and helped provide medical aid.

The Slavery Issue

The Jewish community was largely a northern community. The experience of persecution in Europe had made American

Jews partisans of liberty and usually pitted them against slavery. Three young Jewish immigrants, August Bondi, Jacob Benjamin and Theodore Weiner, were among John Brown's band who fought for abolition of the slave traffic in Kansas in the 1850's. The more established southern Jews, on the other hand, usually of Spanish origin, tended to accept slavery and defended the "peculiar institution." America's two Jewish Senators, Judah P. Benjamin and David Yulee (formerly Levy), favored the slave system. J. F. Moses of Lumpkin, Georgia, an active slave dealer, boasted that he would "warrant every Negro sold to come up to the bill, squarely and completely." Yet other Jews in the South opposed slavery. The New Orleans philanthropist, Judah Touro, freed the one slave he ever owned. Others refused to own slaves at all.

In the North many Jews were abolitionists, though there was no "Jewish position" on slavery. Every Jew and each congregation, in 1860 as much as today, was completely free of hierarchical controls; each was more influenced by its own environment than by religion. Thus, statements by individual Jews represented no more than their own personal opinions. Some rabbis were frightened by the abolitionists and the threat of civil war. Rabbi Issac Mayer Wise, for example, acknowledged that Moses had opposed slavery and had attempted to abolish it, but nonetheless Wise defended the system. He was afraid the abolitionists were not humanitarians interested in helping their fellow men, but politicians bent on securing power. He feared their fanaticism might next be turned against the Jews.

The most publicized of all rabbinical pronouncements on slavery was made just before Lincoln's inauguration by a New York rabbi, Dr. Morris J. Raphall. Raphall's discourse on "The Bible View of Slavery" insisted that the Bible sanctioned human slavery, provided the masters were kind to their slaves. His sermon was reprinted and circulated throughout the country and aroused much attention and controversy.

Some Jews hastened to deny that Raphall spoke for them.

Michael Heilprin, a Philadelphia abolitionist, refuted each of Raphall's contentions. David Einhorn, a rabbi in Baltimore, was even more outspoken. He argued that even in ancient times the abuses inherent in slavery were acknowledged and that Biblical legislation attempted to curb them, proving that slavery was already a recognized evil which would ultimately be abolished. He asked, "Does a disease, perchance, cease to be an evil on account of its long duration?" Einhorn argued that there could be no freedom for any minority in an atmosphere that permitted enslavement of one people by another. Perhaps the strongest Biblical argument against slavery was that God had freed the Israelites from bondage in Egypt, an event of such magnitude that it is celebrated annually at the Passover holiday.

Notwithstanding numerous personal statements by Jews about slavery, Judaism, unlike various Christian denominations, was not a major influence in shaping American opinion prior to the Civil War, and lacking national organizations, it escaped the sectional schisms which developed among Baptists, Methodists, and Presbyterians.

The Chaplaincy Controversy

The United States military chaplaincy originated in colonial times. Until the Civil War it was entirely Protestant. Catholic priests began serving officially as army chaplains at the beginning of the Civil War, but rabbis were still excluded. With Jews enlisting in the Union Army in numbers far greater than in any previous war, and insisting on chaplains of their own faith, the admission of Jews to the chaplaincy became another test of the civil rights theoretically accorded all Americans by the Constitution. In the Confederacy the question never became an issue. There were so few Jewish soldiers in Confederate regiments that no serious demand for Jewish chaplains was felt, and in any case there was no legal barrier to their appointment. In the North, chaplains were required to be "regularly ordained ministers of some Christian denomination." Efforts by Congressman Clement L. Vallandigham of

Rabbi Morris J. Raphall (1798-1868), who defended slavery, provided the masters were kind.

August Bondi (1833-1907), abolitionist who joined John Brown's anti-slavery army in Kansas.

Rabbi David Einhorn (1809-1879), radical Reform leader and outspoken abolitionist.

Army Jews.

The following co-religionists were either killed or wounded at the battle of Fredericksburg:

T. J. Heffernam, A, 163 N. Y., hip and arm.
Serg. F. Herrfukneckt, 7 " head.
M. Ellis, 23 N. J., hand.
Moses Steinburg, 142 Penn., legs bruised.
A. Newman, A, 72 " ankle.
Lt. H. T. Davis, 81 " arm.
J. Killenback, 4 N. J., head.
S. S. Vanuess, 15 " leg.
W. Truax, 23 " back.
J. Hirsh, 4 " "
Jacob Schmidt, 19 Penn., left arm.
Jos. Osback, 19 " wounded.
W. Jabob, 19 " left arm.
Lieut. Simpson, 19 " left leg.
Capt. Schuh, 19 " wounded.
C. M. Phillips, 16 Maine, cheek.
~~Lieut. S. Simpson~~, 99 Penn., leg.
R. Harris, 107 " thigh.

A partial list of Jewish Union soldiers killed or wounded at the Battle of Fredericksburg, December 13, 1862.

List of Soldiers of the Confederate Army buried by George Jacobs. Richmond Va.

Names	Regiment &c	Date of [illegible]	Remarks
Henry Cohen	— 5 6	30th June 1862	Killed in battle
Edwin [illegible]	— Texas	16 July 1862	Killed in battle, 27 June
Jacob A. Cohen	12 Louisiana Regt	29 Sept 1862	" " , 30 Aug
Lewis [illegible]	5 " "	2 May 1863	Died of wound - 1 May 1863
[illegible] J. Levy	46 Va "	23 Aug 1864	Killed in battle 21 Aug 64
Danl Levy	— " "	9 July 1866	Died of Disease contracted

Richmond Va, May 17th 1866.

Mrs R. C. Levy,
Cor. Sec. Heb. Ladies Association &c.
&c. Madame,

Above I hand you the list of Soldiers buried by me during the late war, as requested by the Association, in your letter of 16th inst.

Very respectfully Yours
George Jacobs

A list of Jewish Confederate soldiers buried by the Rev. George Jacobs of Richmond, Virginia.

Michael M. Allen of Philadelphia served as unofficial chaplain of a Pennsylvania Cavalry Regiment in which there were many Jews.

Ohio, in July, 1861, to substitute the phrase "religious society" for the words "Christian denomination" failed. The incident went nearly unnoticed, though Rabbi Wise grasped its significance and praised Vallandigham's effort to correct the "unjust violation of our constitutional rights."

Less than three months later, a Y.M.C.A. worker discovered a Jew, Michael Allen of Philadelphia, serving as the regimental chaplain of the 5th Pennsylvania Cavalry. Horrified, he instigated a public uproar. The commanding officer, Colonel Max Friedman, and a large percentage of the regiment were Jewish, but Allen served in a non-denominational capacity, preaching broad moral concepts and dealing with the down-to-earth problems of men at war: fear, doubt, homesickness, and death. Allen was humiliated and resigned on the excuse of ill health. Colonel Friedman and his officers chose another Jew, the Reverend Arnold Fischel, as Allen's replacement. Fischel immediately applied for a military commission in order to force a test of the issue. As expected, his application was denied.

Jewish organizations began publicizing the grievance. Wise blasted the Republican party for discriminating against Jews, and Isaac Leeser insisted that the whole structure of American democracy was in jeopardy if one class of citizens could so easily be excluded by law from any office. The Jewish press, insisting on equal treatment before the law, called for a united campaign by American Jews. They saw it not as a Jewish matter, but as one affecting all minorities.

Some Protestant groups opposed legal recognition of the equality of the Jewish religion, but the metropolitan newspapers generally supported the Jewish argument for ministers of their own faith. A number of petitions were sent to Congress. Many Christians signed them.

In December, 1861, Fischel went to see Lincoln. The President was very sympathetic. He thought the exclusion of Jewish chaplains had been unintentional on the part of Congress. This was the first Lincoln had heard of the matter and he promised to give it his serious consideration. In July, 1862, the chaplaincy law was changed to permit Catholic, Protestant and Jewish ministers to serve as military chaplains.

Anti-Semitism

Along the battle line between Union and Confederacy in Tennessee, an unsavory and illicit commerce developed as northern speculators, traders, and adventurers rushed to the area to exchange gold and silver, merchandise, and medical supplies for southern cotton, which brought a premium in northern mills. They found men in uniform as eager as themselves to share in the profits. Memphis, Tennessee, became notorious. In Congress it was estimated that twenty to thirty million dollars worth of northern supplies reached the Confederacy through Memphis in a two-year period. General Sherman had even been ordered to encourage the trade but both he and General Grant violently opposed it. Various governmental agencies worked at cross purposes in issuing permits for commercial activity in the area. The result was confusion, leading to bribery and corruption in every branch of the service.

In the midst of this chaos, on December 12, 1862, General Grant issued General Order No. 11, one of the most sweeping anti-Jewish regulations in American history. It called for the expulsion "within twenty-four hours" of "the Jews, as a class," without trial or hearing, from the Department of the Tennessee. Violators would be arrested and held in confinement until they could be shipped out as prisoners. Grant evidently blamed the problem exclusively on the Jewish traders in the area rather than on all the traders who were actually involved.

There was immediate confusion as Jews hurried to leave the area. Cesar Kaskel, one of those expelled, sent letters and telegrams of alarm to Jewish leaders and newspaper editors and went to the capital to see the President, whom he found unaware of the situation and very sympathetic. Lincoln immediately directed the cancellation of the order, and three days later Grant complied.

Many Jews hoped the Senate and House of Representatives would officially oppose the bigotry and prejudice the order stood for, but resolutions in both houses were tabled. The press of the country was divided. Some papers spewed forth anti-Jewish prejudice and bigotry unheard before in America, calling the Jews "the scavengers . . . of commerce." Others, like the *New York Times,* called the order "one of the deepest sensations of the war," and condemned it for "stigmatizing a class, without signalizing the criminals . . ."

Jewish editors, rabbis, and laymen appealed to all Americans to erase this calumny against them. A recurring theme was the anguish of American Jews, condemned as a class, while their rabbis were burying Jewish soldiers killed in battle. The controversy was re-opened when Grant ran for President in 1868 but significantly, no "Jewish vote" emerged. Most American Jews ended up voting according to their stands on the political issues of the day rather than on the memory of Grant's order.

Grant's behavior reflects the ugly truth that people absorb the stereotypes and bigotry of their environment which lie dormant until a severe crisis erupts. Then a scapegoat is sought and prejudice comes to the surface. An unparalleled wave of anti-Semitism, Jew-baiting, and ignorant bigotry spread across the nation as the pressures of war mounted. Grant's wartime attitude toward Jews epitomizes this phenomenon for he never again revealed any antipathy toward Jews. During his presidency he appointed many Jews to public offices. His administration objected to anti-Semitic persecutions in Rumania and Russia. Grant even appointed a Jew as Consul at Bucharest in an effort to pressure the Rumanian government to end its attacks on Jews.

More significant than Grant's order itself and the furor it generated, is the fact that it provoked no physical violence against Jews, nor did it represent a general policy of the government. By contrast, in Europe anti-Semitism was frequently an instrument of government policy. In America, it has rarely been more than an outcropping of bigotry and discrimination under the pressure of a major crisis, or pro-

A SENSATION AT SARATOGA.

June 19, 1877 — N Y Times

NEW RULES FOR THE GRAND UNION.

NO JEWS TO BE ADMITTED—MR. SELIGMAN, THE BANKER, AND HIS FAMILY SENT AWAY—HIS LETTER TO MR. HILTON—GATHERING OF MR. SELIGMAN'S FRIENDS—AN INDIGNATION MEETING TO BE HELD.

On Wednesday last Joseph Seligman, the well-known banker of this City, and member of the syndicate to place the Government loan, visited Saratoga with his wife and family. For 10 years past he has spent the Summer at the Grand Union Hotel. His family entered the parlors, and Mr. Seligman went to the manager to make arrangements for rooms. That gentleman seemed somewhat confused, and said: "Mr. Seligman, I am required to inform you that Mr. Hilton has given instructions that no Israelites shall be permitted in future to stop at this hotel."

Mr. Seligman was so astonished that for some time he could make no reply. Then he said: "Do you mean to tell me that you will not entertain Jewish people?" "That is our orders, Sir," was the reply.

Before leaving the banker asked the reason why Jews were thus persecuted. Said he, "Are they dirty, do they misbehave themselves, or have they refused to pay their bills?"

"Oh, no," replied the manager, "there is no fault to be found in that respect. The reason is simply this: Business at the hotel was not good last season, and we had a large number of Jews here. Mr.

When Joseph Seligman, an outstanding citizen and friend of President Ulysses S. Grant, was turned away from a hotel, the incident became more newsworthy than the common run of anti-Semitic events.

[illegible] ORDERS, } HDQRS. 13TH A. C., DEPT. OF THE TENN.,
[illegible] 11. } *Holly Springs, December* 17, 186[illegible]

The Jews, as a class violating every regulation of trade establish[illegible] by the Treasury Department and also department orders, are here[illegible] expelled from the department within twenty-four hours from the [illegible] of this order.

Post commanders will see that all of this class of people be furnish[illegible] [illegible] and required to leave, and any one returning after such notific[illegible] [illegible] will be arrested and held in confinement until an opportunity [illegible] [illegible] of sending them out as prisoners, unless furnished with perm[illegible] [illegible] headquarters.

[illegible] passes will be given these people to visit headquarters for th[illegible] purpose of making personal application for trade permits.

By order of Maj. Gen. U. S. Grant:

JNO. A. RAWLINS,
Assistant Adjutant-General.

The text of the infamous Order No. 11, issued over the name of General Grant, expelling all Jewish traders from his area. Grant later said he was not responsible for the order, which was cancelled by President Lincoln.

longed social and economic dislocation. This refusal of the government to dabble in anti-Semitism, much less to place its tremendous power at the service of any anti-Semitic program, is not the least of the factors that have made America a New World for the Jews in its midst.

Had the Grant order been the only anti-Semitic incident during the war, it would certainly have been recorded as an isolated aberration. But it was only one example of a series of anti-Jewish libels which became commonplace in both North and South. Verbal attacks against Jews were widespread and common particularly if they were against persons of importance or authority. Judah P. Benjamin, at different times Secretary of State, Attorney General, and Secretary of War in the Confederacy, was regularly slandered by Northern as well as Southern editors. Southern war reverses were often blamed on "that infamous Jew."

In the Confederacy the principal charge against Jews was that of speculating in all manner of merchandise, thereby causing the inflation of the war years. The South had never had an extensive manufacturing base. Heavy wartime demands on industry combined with a successful Union blockade caused severe shortages which drove prices up. Yet there was widespread acceptance of the idea that Jewish merchants were making fortunes exploiting the public, while valiant men were dying on the battlefields. A Jewish stereotype became society's scapegoat. The pattern of bigotry was similar in the North and South. Consciously or unconsciously, libels against Jews provided an escape valve for a people at war.

Post-war Discrimination

Though American anti-Semitism never assumed the virulent forms which at times were prevalent in Europe, and though neither state-sponsored nor privately instigated violence has been a major problem for American Jews, the post-Civil War years witnessed the emergence of the chief forms of anti-Semitism that Jews in America have had to contend with—

discrimination against them in certain jobs, residential areas, social clubs, fashionable resorts, private schools, universities, and professional schools, notably medical schools. Such anti-Semitic discrimination became more pronounced in the 1920's, 1930's, and early 1940's.

However, as early as 1877, the exclusion of Joseph Seligman, the eminent Jewish clothing manufacturer and banker, and his family from a fashionable Saratoga, New York, hotel foreshadowed an evolving pattern of excluding Jews from fashionable resorts. Just when the controversy was waning, the president of the Long Island Railroad bluntly announced, "We do not like the Jews as a class. . . ." This time boycotts were organized and protests were heard again. One interesting result was that the Reverend Henry Ward Beecher, a prominent Protestant minister of the time and a former abolitionist leader, became an outspoken champion of Jewish rights and undoubtedly influenced the attitudes of many Christians.

This incident and the pattern of discrimination it foreshadowed must be seen against a background of the changing social and economic position of American Jews. By 1877, many Jews had become well-to-do merchants. Many were in the professions. Very few were still peddlers or laborers. Jews, more than any other large immigrant group, had become acculturated and had made significant economic gains in the short span of one or two generations. Some had accumulated fortunes and increasing numbers sought admission to higher levels in society which, however, systematically rejected them. For one thing their rapid social rise from humble origins made them abhorrent to high society, and, secondly, significant numbers of eastern European Jews, foreign in language, dress, and manners, were immigrating to America during these same years. These new immigrants undoubtedly stimulated nativist tendencies, and added to the determination of America's social elite to exclude all Jews from their ranks.

Conservative Judaism

The wealthy Jews who were the first victims of social discrimination were, for the most part, members of the Reform wing of American Judaism which by 1885 had deviated in so many ways from traditional Jewish religious practice that traditionalists became alarmed over its growing strength throughout the United States. Out of their defensive reaction to Reform Judaism, the Conservative Jewish movement in America was born. It was built on the traditionalism of Isaac Leeser and his followers, which had already made some compromises with the strictness of Jewish law. Sabato Morais, a Philadelphia rabbi, assumed leadership of the movement. He gained the support of eleven congregations, including the three oldest ones in New York City. In 1886 the Conservative movement founded the Jewish Theological Seminary in New York City and made it clear that while permitting some concessions to the modern world, its basic purpose was to preserve traditional Judaism and to remain "faithful to Mosaic Law and ancestral traditions, for the purpose of keeping alive the true Judaic spirit . . ." The orthodoxy of many of the eastern European Jews, which was to be even more uncompromising in its refusal to depart from traditional Jewish religious practices, took its place at the opposite end of the spectrum from the Reform movement, with Conservative Judaism in the center. These groups still describe the various Jewish affiliations of today. The three, however, do not represent different religions; all the Jews are still regarded as the same people.

The Civil War period hastened the Americanization of thousands of German-Jewish immigrants. The war also unearthed latent anti-Semitism on a scale previously unknown in America. It was revealed in the chaplaincy controversy, in Grant's General Order No. 11, and in a general outbreak of anti-Semitism that continued into the postwar years.

By the end of the century Conservative Judaism had emerged to challenge the preëminence of the Reform move-

3. Read Rabbi Raphall's speech on Biblical slavery and Michael Heilprin's reply in *A Documentary History of the Jews in the U.S.* by Morris U. Schappes, pp. 394-441. (Listed in bibliography of this chapter.) Summarize both arguments. Prepare a script and dramatize the feud.
4. Show a large photograph or picture to the class. Select one that could lend itself to a variety of interpretations. Ask each student to write or tell the story it suggests. Discuss how varying individual backgrounds and points of view frequently lead to different perceptions of the same thing. Ask students to apply the insights that emerge from this discussion by writing an essay on the conflicting American interpretations of the Bible's view of slavery.
5. In what ways was Biblical slavery like the automobile today? (You might say both served their owners, both were subject to regulation by law, etc.) Find a suitable analogy for American slavery, keeping in mind that it was not identical to its Biblical counterpart. (Possibilities: American slavery was like cancer, or it was like an epidemic.) Look for common elements in both parts of your analogy. Be prepared to defend your choice.
6. Was Judah P. Benjamin a good Jew? Divide your research into two parts, the basic requirements of ethical Jewish behavior and Benjamin's life. How would you rate him according to the criteria you establish? What do you think Daniel Webster meant in describing Benjamin as "an Israelite with Egyptian principles?"
7. Write an imaginary letter from Judah Touro, who freed his only slave, to Rabbi George Jacobs of Richmond, Virginia, who maintained slaves in his home. Draw on Biblical references to slavery. (See question 1, above.)
8. Discuss with a rabbi his experiences as a military chaplain. Do the same with a priest or minister. Compare your findings and report to the class.
9. Read and report on Herbert Tarr's delightful book about a Jewish chaplain in the United States Air Force, *The*

Conversion of Chaplain Cohen, Avon Books, New York, 1963. What does it reveal about the experience of being a Jewish chaplain?

10. Write a mock petition to Congress asking that the "unconstitutional and unwise provisions" of the Chaplaincy Act be rescinded immediately. Muster as many arguments as you can. Now, using your experience, write a real petition concerning the mistreatment of any ethnic group in America today. Gather signatures and send it to your senator or congressman.
11. Write a series of newspaper articles or radio scripts in which you tell the story of General Grant's Order No. 11 and its consequences. Invite other students to write letters to the editor concerning your articles or radio broadcasts.
12. Put nine dots on the chalkboard as follows: Ask students to connect all nine dots with four straight strokes without lifting their pencils from the paper.

    Here is the solution:

    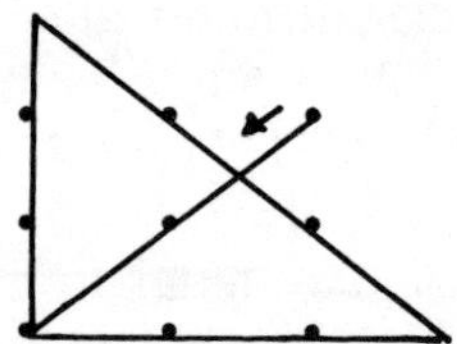

    Examine the "mind-set" which prevented people from seeing it. It involves getting outside the box. Ask: "How is this like stereotyping? How do stereotypes limit one's perceptions?" Have students prepare research reports on how stereotyping influenced opinion about Jews in both North and South during the Civil War.
13. Try an exercise in color metaphors. Colors often char-

acterize feelings, moods, and attitudes. Some are cheerful, others gloomy. Ask students to indicate which color catches the essential quality of each of the following, compare opinions, and ask them to explain their choices. (For example, prejudice might be described as gray, because gray is gloomy and sad, or equality might be seen as yellow, because yellow is happy and cheerful.) Encourage discussion. Add more of your own choice.

prejudice	discrimination	Jew
nativism	freedom	Grant's Order No. 11
equality	civil rights	bigotry
foreigner	anti-Semitism	stereotype

14. Select a Jewish merchant or politician, 1850-1880. Write about his family background, religious training and affiliations, education, and economic and professional endeavors. Describe how the individual you have selected reacted to ongoing American political life.

BIBLIOGRAPHY

Abrahams, Robert D., *Mr. Benjamin's Sword* (Jewish Publication Society, Philadelphia, 1962), is the story of Judah P. Benjamin, the Jewish statesman of the Confederacy. A good biography for young people. Recommended for junior high school readers.

Abrahams, Robert D., *The Uncommon Soldier* (Jewish Publication Society, Philadelphia, 1959). The story of Alfred Mordecai, a Southern-born Jewish cadet at West Point, who must choose between the Union and the Confederacy during the Civil War. Recommended for junior high school students.

Alexander, Lloyd, *Border Hawk* (Farrar, Straus, and Cudahy, New York, 1958). The story of August Bondi and his activities in Kansas before the Civil War. Recommended for junior high school readers.

Dinnerstein, Leonard and Palsson, Mary Dale, (Eds.), *Jews in the South* (Louisiana State University Press, Baton Rouge, 1973). A comprehensive anthology on various aspects of Jewish life in the South from Colonial times to the present. Includes sections on Jewish Life in the Antebellum and Confederate South, Jews in the New South, Southerners View the Jew, Life in the Twentieth-Century South, Jews and Desegregation. For teachers and capable high school students.

Friedman, Lee M., *Pioneers and Patriots* (Jewish Publication Society, Philadelphia, 1955). Chapter 3 is concerned with the chaplaincy controversy. Chapter 23 relates the story of the exclusion of the Seligman family from the Grand Union Hotel in fashionable Saratoga, N. Y. Recommended for teachers and capable high school students.

Huhner, Leon, *Jews in America After the American Revolution* (Gertz Bros., New York, 1959). A collection of essays. "Some Jewish Associates of John Brown," pp. 36-59, is a scholarly, interesting study of John Brown in Kansas. See pp. 60-88 for a good biographical essay on David L. Yulee, Florida's first Jewish senator. Recommended for capable high school students doing research and for teachers seeking background material.

Ish Kishor, Sulamith, *American Promise, A History of the Jews in the New World* (Behrman House, New York, 1947). Chapter 13 deals with the Civil War. Pertinent topics include Biblical interpretations of slavery, Judah P. Benjamin, and Grant's Order No. 11. Recommended for junior high school readers.

Korn, Bertram W., *American Jewry and the Civil War* (Jewish Publication Society, Philadelphia, 1951, and paperback, Meridian Books, Cleveland, 1961). An interesting and scholarly history of the American Jewish community during the Civil War. Dr. Korn provides a wealth of valuable material on topics covered in this chapter, plus many others. Emphasis is on the broad picture, though detail is not ignored. Highly recommended for teachers and capable high school students.

Korn, Bertram W., *Eventful Years and Experiences: Studies in Nineteenth Century Jewish History* (The American Jewish Archives, Cincinnati, 1954). A collection of essays. Chapter 3 deals with the Know-Nothing movement and the Jews. In other chapters he discusses Judah P. Benjamin, the Confederate statesman and Isaac Mayer Wise and the Civil War. Suitable for teachers and capable high school students.

Learsi, Rufus, *The Jews in America: A History* (Ktav Publishing House, Inc., New York, 1972). Chapter 7 deals with the American Jews and the Civil War. It contains a very good section on Grant's Order No. 11. The first part of Chapter 12 deals with anti-Semitism in America in the second half of the nineteenth century. Recommended for teachers and capable high school students.

Levinger, Lee J., *A History of the Jews in the United States* (Union of American Hebrew Congregations, New York, 1961). Chapter 13 provides a good survey of Jewish sympathies during the Civil War. It also contains several pages of biographical material on Judah P. Benjamin. Suitable for junior and senior high school students.

Schappes, Morris U., *A Documentary History of the Jews in the United States, 1654-1875* (The Citadel Press, New York, 1952). Pages 394 through 441 of this source book contain excellent documents on Jews during the Civil War era. "The Slaveholder's Bible" gives the full discourse of Rabbi Morris Raphall in support of slavery; "The Abolitionists' Bible," is the text of Michael Heilprin's reply. The editor's preface to each document is helpful. For teachers and very capable high school students doing research.

Simonhoff, Harry, *Jewish Participants in the Civil War* (Arco Publishing Co., New York, 1963). An excellent book. This and Dr. Korn's scholarly work on American Jewry during the Civil War (see above) are the two major contributions in this field. Simonhoff divides his material into Union and Confederate sections and within each organizes his text around the personalities involved in the war. The book combines solid research with a readable style. Suitable for teachers and high school students.

AUDIO-VISUAL MATERIALS

American Jewry in the Civil War, a filmstrip produced and distributed by the Jewish Education Committee of New York, 426 W. 58th St., New York, N. Y. 10019, 1961. 49 frames, color, includes two copies of narrator's script. This filmstrip deals with American Jewry before and during the Civil War. It depicts organizational and philanthropic efforts of American Jews, and presents conflicting views about slavery. Lacks depth and imagination and will require interpretation and additional information from the teacher. Recommended for high school groups.

The Gift, a kinescope film of the NBC-TV Religious Hour Program, "Frontiers of Faith," produced by the Jewish Theological Seminary of America in cooperation with the National Broadcasting Company, 1956. 30 minutes, black and white. Distributed by the National Academy for Adult Jewish Studies of the United Synagogue of America, 218 E. 70th St., New York, N. Y. 10021. This film is about Judah Touro. It highlights Touro's liberation of his slave and presents conflicting points of view about slavery. Technically it is excellent. The script and acting are also excellent. Suitable for junor and senior high school audiences.

The Jewish Military Chaplain, a filmstrip produced and distriubuted by the Jewish Education Committee of New York, 426 W. 58th Street, New York, N. Y. 10019, 1962. 57 frames, black and white. Includes two copies of narrator's script. The history of the Jewish chaplaincy is reviewed through the use of historic documents and pictures. The photography and script are dull. Emphasis is on the religious function of chaplains. However this filmstrip may have some value as resource material for junior and senior high school students.

Fellow Workers!

Join in rendering a last sad tributè of sympathy and affection for the victims of the Triangle Fire. THE FUNERAL PROCESSION will take place Wednesday, April 5th, at 1 P. M. Watch the newspapers for the line of march.

צו דער לויה שוועסטער און ברידער!

די לויה פון די הייליגע קרבנות פון דעם טרייענגעל פייער וועט זיין מיטוואך, דעם 5טען אפריל, 1 אוהר נאכמיטטאג.

קיינער פון אייך טאר ניט פערבלייבען אין די שעפער! שליסט זיך אן אין די רייהען פון די טרויערענדע! דריקט אויס אייער סימפאטיע און טיעפען בעדויערן איבער דעם גרויסען פערלוסט וואס די ארבייטער־וועלט האט געהאט

געבויגען די קעפ — מיט ציטערנדע הערצער זאלען מיר פיהרען אונזערע טהייערע שוועסטער צו זייער לעצטער רוה.

וואטשט די צייטונגען דורך וועלכע מיר וועלען לאזען וויסען וואו איהר קענט זיך צוזאמענקומען.

צו דער לויה פון די הייליגע קרבנות,
קומט שוועסטער און ברידער!

Operai Italiani!

Unitevi compatti a rendere l'ultimo tributo d'affetto alle vittime dell' imane sciagura della Triangle Waist Co. IL CORTEO FUNEBRE avrà luogo mercoledi, 5 Aprile, alle ore 1 P M. Traverete nei giornali l'ordine della marcia.

A call to join the funeral procession for the victims of the Triangle Shirtwaist Factory fire in 1911. The circular is printed in English, Yiddish and Italian.

CHAPTER VI

THE NEW IMMIGRATION

*

IMPORTANT EVENTS

1881-1882	Pogroms and May Laws introduced in Russia begin new wave of Jewish migration to America.
1881-1924	More than two million eastern European Jews arrive in America.
1900	The International Ladies Garment Workers Union is established.
1903	The Kishinev Massacre in Russia spurs migration to America.
1910	Louis D. Brandeis designs the "Protocol of Peace," ending major garment industry strike.
1914	The Amalgamated Clothing Workers of America is founded.

The Third Wave of Jewish Immigration

Between 1881 and 1924 more than two million eastern European Jews, refugees from hostile governments, poverty, and mass hysteria in Poland and Russia, arrived in America. They constituted the third wave of Jewish migration to the United States, which had actually begun as early as 1870. The German immigration continued until the end of the nineteenth century, but in steadily decreasing numbers. Most of the eastern European Jews came from Russia and regions of Poland ruled by the Czar, although a sizeable number also came from Rumania, Lithuania and Austria-Hungary. The majority of American Jews today are descendants of this group of immigrants, who were far different from the earlier Spanish and German Jews. They were poorer and far less educated and tended to concentrate in large industrial centers where jobs were available. The largest group settled in New York City.

In some years the immigration exceeded 100,000, a staggering number considering that during the Civil War there were only 200,000 Jews in the United States. While the population of the country grew from 50 million to 106 million, a 112% increase, the Jewish community leaped from one-quarter million to three and one-half million, a 1,300% increase. What accounts for this enormous migration of Jews from eastern Europe?

Eastern European Background

At the end of the nineteenth century, Russia, still medieval in her industrial, religious, and governmental development, treated Jews not as Russians or Poles, but as a foreign nation in her midst. Discriminatory laws and special taxes oppressed them and residence restrictions confined them to certain parts of the country known as the Pale of Settlement. They were denied the right to own or rent farms and were the poorest people in a poor nation. Their devotion and loyalty to Judaism were marked by a piety and fervor unknown to their relatively assimilated co-religionists in America.

In March, 1881, Alexander II was assassinated and his son Alexander III became Czar. He feared rebellion by his oppressed subjects and deliberately converted the anger they felt against the government into a patriotic hatred of a common enemy, the Jews, who were blamed for the revolutionary movement and for the poverty of the peasants. Rumors were even circulated that the Jews of Russia were responsible for the assassination of Alexander II. Pogroms began and spread. A pogrom was a mass slaughter of Jews in a given area by peasants and agents of the Czar. Pogroms were essential to the new regime, which planned to force one-third of Russia's Jews to emigrate, one-third to accept baptism, and one-third to be starved to death. Pogroms occurred regularly in Russia until after World War I.

The first year of violence ended with the May Laws of

Polish Jews asking advice about immigrating to the United States, at the information desk of the Hebrew Immigrant Aid Society in Warsaw.

1882 which uprooted thousands from the villages in which they had lived for generations and forced them into already crowded towns and cities where many could not find homes or jobs. They faced discrimination in business, admission quotas in secondary schools and universities, starvation, cholera, and compulsory service in the Czar's army. As late as the early twentieth century insane stories of Jews who sacrificed young Christian boys to use their blood for the celebration of Passover were still circulated and believed.

Confronted with such hysteria and with the oppression of the Czar's government, which more than ever convinced them of their alien status in Russia, many Jews began to seek a way out. Two solutions were at hand. The first sought the establishment of a Jewish state in what was then known as Palestine, a goal that was to be realized in 1948 with the establishment of the State of Israel.* Only a tiny number, however, went to the Holy Land. The second was migration to the United States which appealed to the overwhelming majority.

How much the opportunity to come to the United States meant to these Jews was told by one Russian Jewish immigrant, Mary Antin, in her book, *The Promised Land.* She said,

> So at last I was going to America! Really, really going at last! The boundaries burst. The arch of heaven soared. A million suns shone out for every star. The winds rushed in from outer space, roaring in my ears, 'America, America.'

In April, 1903, the town of Kishinev witnessed a two-day pogrom, leaving forty-seven Jews slain, hundreds injured, and 2,000 families homeless. Reaction was world-wide, but was strongest in the United States where, in pulpit and press, public opinion denounced the incident. In Russia thousands more Jews prepared to leave. More pogroms followed Rus-

* In 1882 a Russian-Jewish physician, Leon Pinsker, had already published a pamphlet, *Auto-Emancipation,* in which he called for "the creation of a Jewish nationality . . . living on its own soil."

sia's defeat in the Russo-Japanese War in 1905 and more Jews left for America.

The migration was also a consequence of America's receptivity to the immigrants. In the years of industrial expansion following the Civil War, growing markets, plentiful capital, and the development of mass production techniques created an atmosphere unusually hospitable to immigration. Workers were needed. The sewing machine and automatic cloth-cutting equipment created a new ready-to-wear clothing industry in which thousands of Jews found jobs.

It was during these years that the saga of the immigrant took shape and became part of American lore. The concept of America as the "mother of exiles" was poignantly expressed by the poet Emma Lazarus, a New York Jew of Spanish ancestry. In 1883 she wrote a sonnet comparing the Statue of Liberty to the Colossus of Rhodes of the Ancient World. It is inscribed on a bronze plaque inside the base of the statue:

THE NEW COLOSSUS

Not like the brazen giant of Greek fame.
With conquering limbs astride from land to land;
Here at our sea-washed, sunset gates shall stand
A mighty woman with a torch, whose flame
Is the imprisoned lightning, and her name
Mother of Exiles. From her beacon-hand
Glows world-wide welcome; her mild eyes command
The air-bridged harbor that twin cities frame.
"Keep, ancient lands, your storied pomp!" cries she
With silent lips. "Give me your tired your poor,
Your huddled masses yearning to breathe free.
The wretched refuse of your teeming shore.
Send these, the homeless, tempest-tost to me.
I lift my lamp beside the golden door!"

The new arrivals met an American-Jewish community of 250,000 acculturated, middle-class German Jews. Many were successful merchants or factory owners or were in the pro-

Emma Lazarus (1849-1887), Jewish poet of New York. In 1883, she wrote the poem, "The New Colossus," which is inscribed on a tablet on the pedestal of the Statue of Liberty in New York harbor.

Jewish tradition was observed even amidst the poverty of the ghetto. This Jew is preparing for the Sabbath in his cellar home.

fessions, and did not wish to be associated with poor, unskilled immigrants whose foreignness and poverty were appalling to them. They feared the ridicule of Christians who might identify all Jews with these bearded, Yiddish-speaking aliens. But they did feel obligated to help the immigrants. They founded the Hebrew Immigrant Aid Society in 1902 and offered the Russian Jews English classes and assistance in finding jobs. They also founded a number of well-organized charitable agencies to help them.

The eastern European Jew left behind the medieval world of eastern Europe which had persistently denied him the most basic economic and political rights. In America he was suddenly transformed into a citizen of a republic, a voter, and a member of a political party. He became part of the most industrialized economy in the world where he had to find a job, a place to live, and adjust to a new way of life. He entered the American economy at a time when its great westward expansion was drawing to a close. But even if this had not been so, he was too poor to afford the opportunities the West offered. In 1900 the average Jewish immigrant arrived in America with $9. The figure for immigrants, in general, was $15. Therefore he usually remained in the large urban centers of the East. A small number, aided by the Hebrew Immigrant Aid Society and similar agencies did locate elsewhere in the country.

The Jewish Labor Movement

The vast majority of eastern European Jews settled in New York and a few other large metropolitan areas, in what were to become predominantly Jewish neighborhoods. They lived in the older slum sections where rent was cheap and the tenements crowded and filthy. Some Jews became pushcart peddlers, shop owners, laborers, housepainters, butchers, tailors, glaziers, shoemakers, carpenters, and clerks, and a few were professionals. Some, like Samuel Gompers, later president of the American Federation of Labor, entered new trades like cigar making. The largest number of Jews were employed in the garment industry, for a variety of reasons. It was a field in which many had already worked before leaving Russia,* and the industry was concentrated in New York City, the principal port of entry for immigrants. This was an important factor to a people of extremely limited resources, as was the simple fact that it took no capital to become a garment worker. Moreover, the owners of the garment factories were often German Jews, willing to employ the immigrant Jews from eastern Europe.

Working conditions in the garment industry were terrible. From about 1880 to 1910 the principal evil was the "contract system" and the abominable sweatshops it spawned. Most manufacturers employed only cutters, whose output was bundled and delivered to contractors who produced the finished garments in their own shops. The competition was fierce, and contractors regularly exploited their workers. Despite the cruelty of the system, the contractors were as much its victims as any. They frequently used their own tenement flats as shops by day and living quarters by night. Most sweatshops were dangerous, dark, airless, unsanitary firetraps. Often whole families worked to help meet quotas. Tuberculosis and other diseases were rampant. Workers might begin at four in the morning and work until ten at night. Men earned six to ten dollars a week, and women and children much less. Many provided their own sewing machines and were forced to pay for the electricity they consumed. If a worker complained, shiploads of immigrants waited to take his place.

Such conditions led Jews to join the labor union movement. In 1888 the United Hebrew Trades was formed in New York by Russian-Jewish intellectuals imbued with a strong social consciousness. Though it failed, it was through it and similar associations in other cities that Jewish immigrants made their first contact with organized labor.

Strong unions did not emerge in the garment industry

* The Russian census of 1897 reported that almost one-fifth of Russian Jews in cities over 100,000 in population, were in the clothing industry.

A sweatshop on Ludlow Street in New York City. A Hebrew wedding certificate hangs on the wall. Tenement flats were used as shops during the day and as living quarters at night.

until after the turn of the century when workers and their leaders joined the American Federation of Labor. Two predominantly Jewish labor unions which were to dominate the clothing industry were the International Ladies Garment Workers (ILGWU), led by David Dubinsky, and the Amalgamated Clothing Workers of America, led by Sidney Hillman. Well organized strikes by these unions exposed conditions to the public and pushed the employers to negotiate for improvement. One such strike in 1910 was settled by a famous labor-management agreement designed by a Boston lawyer named Louis Dembitz Brandeis, later a justice of the Supreme Court. It established a permanent board of arbitration, a grievance committee, and a joint board of sanitary control. It became a model for other labor agreements.

The Triangle Shirtwaist Factory fire in 1911, which claimed the lives of nearly one hundred and fifty people, most of them young Jewish women, pointed tragically to the need for better working conditions. Over the years, the International and the Amalgamated worked to improve unsanitary and dangerous conditions in the industry. They won recognition as the official bargaining agents of the workers. Wages went up, hours went down, and child labor was eliminated. These Jewish unions pioneered in constructive employer-employee relations. They earned the right of collective bargaining and insisted on written contracts. They helped develop new techniques for impartial arbitration of labor disputes and broke new ground in establishing fringe benefits for their members. Social, educational, and health services were established, as were classes, lectures, picnics, nurseries, housing developments, college scholarships, camps, summer resorts, dances, concerts, banks, unemployment insurance and pensions.

Over the years, the International and the Amalgamated suffered from many of the problems which have plagued trade unions in general—racketeering, communist penetration, and the problems of sheer size. None of these, however, has diminished their remarkable record. The steady exodus of Jewish workers from the garment factories since the end of

World War I has led to the predominance of other ethnic groups in the industry. At mid-century only twenty-eight percent of the Amalgamated and the International were Jewish. But whatever the ethnic composition of the industry, the legacy of the once largely Jewish unions and their trail-blazing accomplishments remains an important chapter in American labor history.

Politics

Some of the Jews who migrated to America did so as convinced socialists. Their attitude was not a rejection of America, which politically was still unknown to them, but a rejection of the political oppression they had faced in Russia and other parts of eastern Europe. Some migrated to America with the intention of building a socialist utopia on these shores. It was Jews of such background who in 1901 helped form the Socialist Party in the United States and in 1912 organized the Jewish Socialist Federation as its Jewish section. However, in the relatively hospitable political climate of America, Jewish socialism was increasingly irrelevant, and it soon became a relic of the immigrant generation. Within a few short years, American Jews were indistinguishable from their Democratic or Republican fellow-Americans. The efforts of these early socialists, Jewish and non-Jewish, were, however, by no means futile, for the reforms they advocated were later to be adopted by the New Deal and subsequent administrations.

Religious Life

The first generation of eastern European Jews created a far more extensive organized Jewish life than had the German Jews before them. They founded Jewish schools, community centers, newspapers, theaters, clubs and literary societies. In the free climate of America they acculturated gradually. But they were unwilling to live an entirely sectarian life. The immigrants became proud citizens, voted regularly, sent their children to public school, and went to night school themselves, but nonetheless, they did maintain a uniquely Jewish world.

In 1877 there were 227 Jewish congregations in the United States. Nearly all were Reform temples. In 1900 there were 850 congregations, most of them Orthodox. The change is accounted for by the influx of half a million Jewish immigrants whose ranks included large numbers of pious Jews. Orthodox congregations proliferated, often beginning in ill-furnished quarters in buildings occupied by sweatshops. Frequently they were made up of people from the same community in Europe.

Conservative Judaism, meanwhile, was a failure. By 1897 more than half of the original membership had abandoned it, and with the death of its leader, Sabato Morais, its future was bleak. But the arrival of half a million East European Jews by the end of the century drastically altered the situation and gave new life to the movement. Some of these immigrants had already shed their orthodoxy in Europe. In America others hastened to join them. The rate of attrition, particularly among the native born young, was frightening to the older generation of the Orthodox. The Conservative movement now recognized its potential appeal to those who, even if no longer Orthodox, were unwilling to forsake entirely the traditional forms of religion in which they had been raised. Conservative Judaism, despite certain compromises in ritual, had never altered the central core of Jewish law, as had Reform Judaism. Theologically it was still closely related to Orthodoxy and it attracted members from the new generation, the children of the immigrants. The Jewish Theological Seminary of America was revitalized with Solomon Schechter, a renowned Jewish scholar, as its president. In time Conservative membership grew, attracting large numbers of second and third generation eastern European Jews.

Despite the inroads of Conservatism and the abandonment of traditional religious practice by many of the immigrants and even more of their descendants, Orthodox Judaism has won a permanent place for itself on the American scene. Its ranks were augmented after World War II by the arrival of thousands of Orthodox Jews from eastern Europe, who settled for the most part in New York City.

Jewish Education

When the eastern European Jews began arriving after 1880 there was no meaningful Jewish educational system in America, except Sunday schools that met a few hours per week. Earlier efforts of the German Jews to maintain Jewish day schools had failed in the 1850's partly as a result of the competition of public schools. The eastern European Jews established supplementary religious schools of their own which held classes in the late afternoon, after public school, and on Sunday mornings. Such one-room schools sprouted by the hundreds in the Jewish neighborhoods of large cities after 1880, offering instruction in the Hebrew language, the prayer book, and the Bible. Soon more professional schools called *Talmud Torahs* took their place. They attempted to serve a larger number of students distributed in graded classes. They charged tuition and were supported by the Jewish community at large. Some students attended all-day Jewish schools, studying both religious and secular subjects. Teacher-training institutions, such as Gratz College in Philadelphia, were founded. In the field of higher education, the *yeshiva* (institute of higher learning) was founded. The most famous was the Isaac Elhanan Theological Seminary in New York, which became the nucleus of Yeshiva University.

These schools reached only a small percentage of Jewish children. One survey in 1908 showed that only 28% of Jewish children between the ages of six and sixteen received any Jewish education at all. Many of the immigrants and their children were ambivalent in their attitudes to their tradition. They were eager on one hand to escape from it and become Americanized, but determined on the other to perpetuate their heritage. Many were too eager for their children to master the English language and to receive a secular education, and too preoccupied by the effort to escape their poverty to make a more sustained and successful attempt to provide a Jewish education for their children. Such an effort had to wait for the very different material conditions and social attitudes which prevailed in the years after World War II.

Social and Cultural Associations

The eastern European Jews were as displeased with the network of Jewish social and cultural associations which greeted them as they had been with the inadequate system of Jewish education that they found. They promptly created a host of organizations to meet a variety of social and cultural needs. Settlement Houses were begun in Jewish neighborhoods and "Young Men's Benevolent Associations" abounded, ministering to the social and recreational needs of their members. There were two major reasons for the rise of such societies. For one thing, the older established organizations, founded by the German Jews, tended to be remote and unreceptive. Secondly, many of the societies and associations they created derived their impetus from a nostalgic need to share memories of home with former countrymen and to stand together against the imagined or real vulnerability of strangers in a new land. They became havens to which the confused immigrants could turn for comfort and support during the difficult years of settling into a new life.

Yiddish

Yiddish was the language of the eastern European Jewish immigrants. In America Jews developed Yiddish literature and a Yiddish press. Daily newspapers in Yiddish were most successful in New York City, which had four in 1930, though notable efforts were also made in Chicago, Cleveland, Philadelphia and Milwaukee. Some equalled the English dailies in content and coverage. Outside New York Yiddish weeklies succeeded. There were also monthly journals and the

Yiddish theater was an early part of immigrant life in the United States. It attained a high literary and dramatic level. Above, a poster advertising a Yiddish production.

country saw a remarkable growth of Yiddish fiction, poetry, and drama.

The Yiddish press reflected the social and intellectual life of the immigrants. It reported the general news and provided a forum for social, political, literary, and scientific discussions. It explained American history and government to the new immigrant in the only language he could understand. Abraham Cahan's *Jewish Daily Forward* exposed the evils of tenements and sweatshops, gave newcomers information about their new country, and encouraged naturalization, voting, and interest in civic affairs.

Yiddish was important in a number of other ways. Many immigrants continued reading Yiddish fiction in America. Sholom Aleichem is best known to this generation of Americans for his stories which inspired the Broadway musical and motion picture, *Fiddler on the Roof*. Yiddish theater, too, was an early part of immigrant life in the United States. It attained a high literary and dramatic level and far exceeded anything ever done on the Yiddish stage in Europe.

Hebrew language publications, unlike those in Yiddish, were generally unsuccessful. Hebrew is the liturgical and scholarly language of Jews, not the language of everyday life. It is only since 1948, with the founding of the State of Israel, that Hebrew has been given widespread consideration as a second language among American Jews. Courses in modern Hebrew are offered in a growing number of high schools and universities, though very few American Jews have a practical mastery of it.

By mid-twentieth century the Yiddish theater and the Yiddish press were on the wane. With large scale immigration over, the audiences needed to sustain them were lacking. The Yiddish language fell into disuse. Gifted writers like Fannie Hurst, Ludwig Lewisohn, Waldo Frank, Edna Ferber, Ben Hecht, Michael Gold, Abraham Cahan and others wrote about the Jewish experience in English. The shift from Yiddish to English was an indication that the eastern European Jews had been Americanized in the short span of one or two generations. Nevertheless, many American Jewish writers have never lost their affection for the language of their parents and grandparents. Such noted writers and critics as Saul Bellow and Irving Howe have been active as translators and editors of Yiddish literature, and one contemporary Yiddish writer, Isaac Bashevis Singer, has won a considerable number of readers for the English translations of his short stories and novels.

Jews in Music

The immigrants and their children proved especially talented as composers and musicians and they took to America with a passion, so much so that they played an important role in creating some of the most typically American forms of music and musical theatre.

American Jews have been particularly active as composers of Broadway musicals. Most of these shows have long since been forgotten, but a few have become classics of the American theatre. Jerome Kern, born in New York in 1885, took a novel by Edna Ferber and in 1927 turned it into a musical called *Show Boat.* Irving Berlin, the son of a cantor who immigrated to New York when the boy was five, grew up on New York's lower East Side and became a prolific writer of popular songs. Better known and more talented by far was George Gershwin, born in Brooklyn in 1898, who wrote *Porgy and Bess* and *An American in Paris* and was one of the first composers to adapt jazz to more traditional forms in the *Rhapsody in Blue* and *Concerto in F.* Richard Rodgers has been a prolific composer of Broadway scores, among them *Oklahoma* and *South Pacific*. The contributions of American Jews to the native idiom has continued to the present day in the work of such composers and lyricists as Bob Dylan, Paul Simon, and Art Garfunkel.

Older and more venerable still, however, is the contribution which American Jews have made to the great tradition of Western music. For more than 150 years Jews have been preëminent among the world's great performing musicians, and the American representatives of this tradition include the violinists Jascha Heifetz, Nathan Milstein, Erica Morini, and Isaac Stern; the pianists Vladimir Horowitz, Rosalyn Tureck, Artur Rubinstein, and Rudolph Serkin; the cellists Emanuel Feuermann, Gregor Piatigorsky, Raya Garbousova, and Leonard Rose; the singers Robert Merrill, Richard Tucker, Beverly Sills, and Jan Peerce. Most of these men and women were born in eastern Europe, but have made their careers in the United States. Some, such as Isaac Stern, were brought to this country as infants; others came as mature artists.

Historically, Jews have been far less prominent as composers than performers, but in the twentieth century they have made important contributions to composition, as well. American examples include Ernest Bloch (1880-1959), Aaron Copland, and Leonard Bernstein, each of whom has drawn in their compositions both on American themes and on the Jewish tradition, especially as it is embodied in the Scriptures and in the liturgy. Bloch, who was born in Switzerland, but settled in America in 1917, wrote *America,* an epic rhapsody for chorus and orchestra, as well as *Schelomo,* a rhapsody for cello and orchestra inspired by the Biblical portrait of King Solomon, the *Israel Symphony,* and a setting of the Sabbath liturgy, *Sacred Service.* In *Billy the Kid, Rodeo,* and *Appalachian Spring,* Aaron Copland has written classic American ballet scores; he has also written *Vitebsk,* a trio for violin, cello, and piano based on Jewish themes. The tradition is maintained by perhaps the most notable of contemporary American composers, Leonard Bernstein, the first American-born musician to serve as Music Director and Conductor of the New York Philharmonic. Bernstein has written *West Side Story, Fancy Free, On the Town,* and *Wonderful Town,* as well as compositions inspired by Hebrew Bible and liturgy, such as the *Jeremiah Symphony, Kaddish,* an oratorio which makes use of the Hebrew prayer for the dead from which the title of the work derives, and the *Chichester Psalms.*

TO THE TEACHER:

This chapter brings the eastern European Jews to America. Their arrival is important for the themes of immigration, pluralism, urbanization, and the labor movement, and is part of what historians call the "new immigration," which, after 1880, brought millions of people to the United States from southern and eastern Europe, as contrasted to the "old" immigrants who came principally from northern and western Europe. It is not suggested that the new immigration be dealt with solely in terms of the Jewish experience. On the contrary, because eastern European Jews shared in the migration with numerous other minorities, they should be included with them in general accounts of the movement. Their flight from the murderous pogroms of the Czar was unique, but otherwise their experience paralleled that of the millions of Italians, Greeks, Austro-Hungarians, Bulgarians, Rumanians and Turks who also came, seeking freedom and economic opportunity.

In one respect, however, the experience of the Jewish immigrant did differ from that of his non-Jewish counterparts. In Russia and Poland, the Jews were treated as a separate nation, but in a discriminatory and invidious manner. They were segregated in the Pale of Settlement, but possessed no national homeland of their own; they were treated as a foreign element in the body politic, denied the rights (such as they were) enjoyed by their fellow Russians and Poles, and yet expected to pay taxes to and fight for the authorities under whose sway they lived. Jews were only too eager to escape these conditions and this, among other factors, explains why, as noted in this chapter, American Jews refused to establish here the partly self-governing religious communities they had known in Europe. Such communities were associated in their minds with the denial of civic rights for Jews in the larger community. (Of course, other factors were also at work. The American doctrine of separation of church and state meant that each religious community was a voluntary association which could not, in any case, exercise coercive powers over its adherents.)

These considerations suggest several themes for class discussion. The teacher might begin by asking, "Can a nation survive without a land of its own?" The discussion might attempt to define the characteristics of a nation. The focus might be shifted to more immediate concerns of students, such as nationalism, ethnic identity, and the extent to which a nation has the right to demand obedience to established laws, payment of taxes, and rendering of military service on the part of its minority citizens if it consigns them to a condition of civic inferiority.

The ethnic mixture created by the new immigration soon became identified with urban growth, as millions of newcomers crowded into large industrial cities seeking work. Eastern European Jews were central to the process of urbanization. Their experience not only epitomizes the movement as they crowded into the teeming neighborhoods of first settlement, but is so basic to any study of the labor movement that its inclusion is essential. The so-called Jewish labor unions, largely in the garment industry, were pioneers in advancing the process of collective bargaining and in creating employee health, recreational, and welfare plans; yet, surprisingly, this fact is neglected in most American history courses. The concentration of Jews in the garment industry illustrates another facet of American economic history which is generally overlooked. Not all immigrants went to work in the steel mills and heavy industries of America. Millions of others were employed in the needle trades or were engaged in other light industries where working conditions were appalling and poverty was a constant factor.

Some Jews, having been influenced by radical thought in eastern Europe, became active in the Socialist party in America, through which they sought to alleviate the conditions of the poor. The Socialist party anticipated numerous reforms which were later accepted by the Democratic and Republican parties. This provides an opportunity for a discussion of the role of minority parties in American political history. The minority party, precisely because it lacks a mass following which it must cater to and conciliate, and because the relatively small following that it does have is ideologically committed and homogeneous, is free to advocate programs and policies which at first are shunned by the established parties.

The emergence of Conservative Judaism at the end of the nineteenth century, as a defensive reaction to the Reform movement suggests the concept of social change and invites discussion of cause and effect and stimulus and response in history. Moreover, the appeal of Conservative Judaism to the children of the Orthodox immigrants suggests a more general pattern in which the children of the immigrants, influenced by the new environment, broke with many of the older traditions.

The network of cultural, educational, and religious organizations which the eastern European Jews created, symbolized the multi-ethnic structure of American society and contradicted the melting-pot theory long before its demise was recognized by scholars and teachers. The disinclination of the eastern European Jewish immigrant to assimilate completely, while, nonetheless, cherishing the opportunities that came with being American (especially for his children), made for a plurality of cultures in America and is central to an understanding of the immigrant generation and its problems.

DISCUSSION QUESTIONS AND STUDENT ACTIVITIES

1. Prepare a chart depicting the three "waves" of Jewish immigration to the United States, Spanish, German and eastern European. For each explain:
   A) Why immigrants came
   B) From where they came
   C) Whether they were unique as Jews or part of a general migration including non-Jews, as well
   D) Where they settled
   E) What jobs they took
   F) Lasting contributions to the Jewish community
   G) Lasting contributions to American life
   H) Outstanding members of the migration
   I) Immigration laws in force at the time they came.

2. Make a bar chart or graph for the class bulletin board showing Jewish population growth in the United States since 1790. A good starting point might be *A History of the Jews in the United States* by Lee J. Levinger, pp. 262-64 (listed in Basic Bibliography). Make comparative population charts for other ethnic groups.
3. In the periodicals sections of a large library look up newspaper accounts of the Kishinev massacre in April, 1903. Report your findings to the class.
4. Discuss the play, *Fiddler on the Roof*. Ask a student who has seen the movie or show to summarize it, or have students read the play. To what extent does it inform you about the life of the poor Jew in Russia? What led him to migrate to the United States? How does anti-Semitism in Russia today compare or contrast to anti-Semitism in the years before the Russian Revolution? To what extent is life accurately portrayed in the play? To what extent is it romanticized?
5. Read and report on Leon Pinsker's *Auto-Emancipation*. Compare it to other nationalistic movements of the nineteenth and twentieth centuries.
6. The poem, "Mother of Exiles," by Emma Lazarus, has been set to music. Have students use a recording of it as the soundtrack for a slide show or movie. Refer to the poem, itself, for ideas about what to film. Prepare a script beforehand, listing all the scenes or slides to be taken. Edit the film or slide show to synchronize with the sound-track.
7. Have students read and report to the class on:

   Antin, Mary, *The Promised Land*. Tell the class why her family left Russia, what their life was like in the U.S., and how Mary took advantage of the American educational system.

   Malamud, Bernard, *The Fixer*. Describe the blood accusations and other bizarre persecutions that led Jews to leave Russia.

   Metzker, Isaac, *A Bintel Brief*. What do the letters in

this book tell you about life on the Lower East Side of New York? Is the picture of life complete in this book?

8. Write an original play depicting working conditions in the garment industry around the turn of the century. Be sure to include the evils of the contract system.
9. Describe the average day and working conditions of a Jewish worker in the garment industry in the 1890's or early 1900's. Describe your parents' working day. Compare salary, hours, standard of living, vacations, unemployment compensation, insurance, medical care, plant safety, union benefits, grievance procedures, pension.
10. Write to the educational departments of the Amalgamated Clothing Workers of America and the International Ladies Garment Workers Union for information on the history of these unions and current health, welfare, housing, and recreational programs. Their addresses are:

    International Ladies Garment Workers Union
    1710 Broadway
    New York, N. Y. 10019

    Amalgamated Clothing Workers of America
    15 Union Square
    New York, N. Y. 10003
11. Prepare an outline of the history of the labor movement in the United States, including the role of the Jewish labor unions.
12. Report on two major strikes in the garment industry, "The Uprising of the 20,000" and "The Great Revolt." Be sure to include the role of Louis D. Brandeis and the "Protocol of Peace."
13. In the periodicals section of a large library look up newspaper accounts of the Triangle Shirtwaist Company fire of March, 1911. Report your findings to the class.
14. Prepare a biographical report on any of the following:

Louis D. Brandeis	Samuel Gompers
Abraham Cahan	Sidney Hillman
David Dubinsky	Morris Hillquit

15. Make a comparative reading report on two novels related to the Jewish immigrant experience, *The Rise of David Levinsky* by Abraham Cahan and *Call It Sleep* by Henry Roth. (Both are listed in the bibliography of this chapter.)
16. Using source books and current magazine articles, write comparative descriptions of Jewish ghettos in New York at the beginning of the twentieth century and Black ghettos in large American cities today.
    Enumerate and describe similarities and differences.
    How do you account for the differences?
    What could the U.S. government do to help eradicate poverty in all ethnic ghettos today?
17. Do a research report on the role of Jews in the socialist movement in the United States. You might start by looking up material on Victor Berger of Milwaukee or Morris Hillquit of New York.
18. Interview a rabbi or do some independent research to learn why Jews continued to study the Bible and Talmud throughout most of their exile. How extensively is it studied today?
19. Have students read and report on literature by Jewish authors. Some examples are:

Sholom Aleichem	Arthur Miller
Mary Antin	I. L. Peretz
Sholom Asch	Chaim Potok
Saul Bellow	Leo Rosten
Abraham Cahan	Henry Roth
Edna Ferber	I. J. Singer
Laura Hobson	Irwin Shaw
Alfred Kazin	Leon Uris
Ludwig Lewissohn	Herman Wouk
Bernard Malamud	Israel Zangwill

20. Play a recording of the song "Tradition" from *Fiddler on the Roof*. Institutions like the family and the village stand out. Analyze how they have helped shape Jewish

life and Jewish values. What institutions influence you in your daily life?

21. Browse through Leo Rosten's delightful book, *The Joys of Yiddish*, Pocket Books, New York, 1970. Make a list of Yiddish words (all are written in English) which you hear in everyday English.
22. Conduct a "music festival" in your class. Have students bring in and play recordings of some of the music by Jewish composers mentioned in this chapter.

BIBLIOGRAPHY

Antin, Mary, *The Promised Land* (Houghton Mifflin Company, Boston, Second Edition, 1969). Autobiography of a Russian Jewish girl who came to the United States. Originally written in 1911. Illustrates the role of free education in helping poor immigrants improve their status. Foreward by Oscar Handlin. For high school students and capable junior high students.

Cahan, Abraham, *The Rise of David Levinsky* (Harper & Row, paperback, New York, 1966). Recreates life in the lower East Side. Deals with problems of assimilation, adjustment, and success in the American environment. Set in the ready-to-wear garment industry. A classic in immigrant literature, by the editor of the *Jewish Daily Forward*. For high school students or capable junior high students.

Davis, Moshe, *The Emergence of Conservative Judaism* (Jewish Publication Society, Philadelphia, 1963). A study of the historical evolution and adaptation of Judaism to the American environment. Part II traces the growth of Reform Judaism from which sprang the Conservative "counter reform" movement. Suitable for teachers and capable high school students.

Friedman, Theodore, and Gordis, Robert, (Eds.), *Jewish Life in America* (Horizon Press, New York, 1955). An anthology of the Jewish religion and culture. "Secularism and Religion in the Jewish Labor Movement," by C. Bezalel Sherman, pp. 109-127, is an interesting essay on the Jewish trade union movement. "The East Side: Matrix of the Jewish Labor Movement," by Abraham Menes, pp. 131-154, deals with immigration, the garment industry, and the Jewish labor movement, with emphasis on values among Jewish workers. Both essays are suitable for teachers and high school students.

Gay, Ruth, *Jews in America* (Basic Books, New York, 1965). Chapter 3, "Golden Land," is an interesting summary of the "Russian" migration, stressing the eastern European background and the cultural and economic life of the immigrants. Suitable for teachers and junior and senior high school students.

Glazer, Nathan, *American Judaism* (University of Chicago Press, Second Edition, Chicago, 1972, also in paperback). Chapters 3 and 4 describe the emergence of a strong Conservative Jewish religious movement in America as a reaction to the growth of Reform Judaism and the arrival of Orthodox eastern European Jews after 1880. Chapter 6 deals with the movement of eastern European Jewish immigrants to areas of second settlement and the social and cultural adjustments entailed in the process. The material is suitable for teachers and the most capable high school students.

Glazer, Nathan, and Moynihan, Daniel Patrick, *Beyond the Melting Pot* (M.I.T. Press, Cambridge, 1963). Comparisons of Jews, Blacks, Italians, Puerto Ricans and Irish in New York City. For teachers and capable high school students.

Gold, Michael, *Jews Without Money* (Avon paperback, New York, 1968). A classic novel of urban social protest, originally published in 1930. Vividly depicts immigrant poverty on New York's lower East Side. Particularly useful in urban affairs courses. This edition includes an "afterword" by Michael Harrington. Recommended for high school students.

Gould, Jean, *Sidney Hillman, Great American* (Houghton Mifflin Co., Boston, 1952). A sympathetic biography of an important labor leader. Recommended for junior high school students.

Handlin, Oscar, *Adventure in Freedom: Three Hundred Years of Jewish Life in America* (McGraw-Hill, New York, 1954). Chapter 5 is an excellent discussion of the eastern European immigrants and their settlement in America. Professor Handlin is particularly good on Jews in large cities and in the garment industry. Chapter 6 describes the cultural and religious characteristics of the eastern European Jewish immigrants, who are contrasted with the more established German-Jewish community. Chapter 7 deals with the Americanization of the eastern European immigrants and their gradual acceptance by the German-Jews. The treatment is very thorough. Recommended for teachers and capable high school students.

Hapgood, Hutchins, *The Spirit of the Ghetto: Studies of the Jewish Quarter of New York* (Funk and Wagnalls, New York, 1965, also in paperback). A remarkable work written by a non-Jew in 1902 who records his sensitive and perceptive observations of New York's Jewish quarter. The preface and running commentary are by Harry Golden. The book is illustrated by the famous sculptor, Sir Jacob Epstein. Highly recommended for teachers and high school students.

Herberg, Will, "The Jewish Labor Movement in the U.S.," in *American Jewish Yearbook,* Vol. 53 (Jewish Publication Society, Philadelphia, 1952). A scholarly article tracing the history of the Jewish trade-union movement from the late nineteenth century to the mid-twentieth century. Discusses political and social aspects of the movement. Recommended primarily for teachers and capable high school students doing research.

Kurtis, Arlene Harris, *The Jews Helped Build America* (Julian

Messner, New York, 1970). A short book (95 pages) written at the upper elementary level. It includes material on various topics but concentrates on the eastern European immigrants, the contemporary Jewish community, and Jewish contributors to America. Ideal for any secondary school student with reading difficulties. The material is mature, but the reading level is 4th to 6th grade. Well illustrated which should further enhance its appeal for slow readers.

Learsi, Rufus, *The Jews in America: A History* (Ktav Publishing House, Inc., New York, 1972). The relevant chapters here are: 9, The cultural background of eastern European Jewry as of the year 1891; 11, the story of immigrant Jewish labor and the Jewish labor movement; 12 (second half), the early Zionist movement which emerged in Europe around the turn of the century; 13, the three languages which the immigrants used, Yiddish, Hebrew, and English. Suitable for teachers and capable high school students.

Levinger, Lee J., *A History of the Jews of the United States* (Union of American Hebrew Congregations, New York, 1961). Chapter 18, "Cultural Institutions of the Russian Jews," deals with many of the topics covered in this chapter. Chapter 25 is a good survey of the Jewish religion in America. Suitable for junior and senior high school students.

Merrian, E., *The Voice of Liberty: The Story of Emma Lazarus* (Farrar, Straus & Cudahy, New York, 1959). The story of Emma Lazarus, the poet whose "New Colossus" is mounted on a plaque at the base of the Statue of Liberty. For junior high school readers.

Metzker, Isaac, (Ed.), *A Bintel Brief* (Doubleday, Garden City, 1971). Also in paperback, Ballantine Books, New York. A cross section of letters to the editor of New York's leading Jewish newspaper, the *Jewish Daily Forward*. The letters, sometimes humorous, sometimes sad, offer a personal commentary on the adjustment of eastern European Jews to American life. The book contains excellent photographs. Recommended for junior and senior high school students.

Pessin, Deborah, *History of the Jews in America* (United Synagogue of America, New York, 1957). Unit IV, Chapter 3, parallels much of this chapter. It emphasizes cultural, organizational, and religious aspects of early immigrant life. Recommended for junior high school students.

Riis, Jacob, *How the Other Half Lives* (Hill & Wang, New York, 1957). Paperback. Originally published in 1902, the book vividly portrays life in New York tenements during the late nineteenth century. In 1870, Riis emigrated from Denmark to the United States, where he became a journalist, photographer, and reformer. Theodore Roosevelt called Riis "the most useful citizen of New York," and this account of tenement life reflects the author's sensitivity and social conscience. Recommended for high school students.

Rischin, Moses, *The Promised City: New York's Jews, 1870-1914* (Harvard University Press, Cambridge, 1962). Paperback: Corinth Books, 1964. Describes the problems, adjustments, and gratifications of Jewish immigrants in New York City. The author discusses the economic and social life of the immigrants, explains trade unionism, and contrasts Yiddish culture with the American environment. Recommended for teachers and advanced high school students.

Roth, Henry, *Call It Sleep* (Pageant Books, Paterson, N. J., 1960.) Also paperback, Avon Books, New York, 1964. Originally published in 1934. A vivid picture of the Jewish immigrant experience. Language and style are difficult. Recommended for teachers and capable high school students.

St. John, Robert, *Jews, Justice and Judaism* (Doubleday, New York, 1969). Chapters 15 and 17 deal with the Russian background of the eastern European migration. Chapter 18 includes, among other things, a good discussion of the Protocols of the Elders of Zion. Chapter 20 is about the

Jewish labor movement. Recommended for teachers and high school students.

Schappes, Morris U., *The Jews in the United States, A Pictorial History* (Citadel Press, New York, 1958). Chapters 9 and 10 of this superbly illustrated volume are pertinent here. Chapter 9 deals with the eastern European immigration. Chapter 10 is particularly good on the Jewish labor movement. In both, the Jewish material is smoothly integrated into general history, particularly in the case of the reform movements of the Progressive era. Excellent for both junior and senior high school students, as well as for teachers.

Schoener, Allon, *Portal to America: The Lower East Side 1870-1925* (Holt, Rinehart and Winston, 1967). Also in paperback. Depicts New York's Lower East Side as the gateway through which millions of immigrants entered a new life in America. Portrays the Lower East Side as an environment of aspiration and achievement, and documents the contributions of many famous Jewish Americans who grew up in the area. A vivid and interesting book, including reprints of newspaper articles and photographs. Recommended for all readers.

Wirth, Louis, *The Ghetto* (University of Chicago Press, Chicago, 1928, and paperback, Phoenix Books, Chicago, 1956). This is a solid study of the ghetto and its sociological significance. Chapters 1 through 7 deal with the European ghetto. Chapters 9, 10, and 11 provide a study of the eastern European Jewish community of Chicago. Recommended for teachers and capable high school students.

AUDIO-VISUAL MATERIALS

Between Two Eternities, a kinescope film from the NBC-TV Religious Hour Program, "Frontiers of Faith," produced by the Jewish Theological Seminary of America in cooperation with the National Broadcasting Company, 1953. 30 minutes, black and white. Distributed by the National Academy for Adult Jewish Studies of the United Synagogue of America, 218 E. 70th St., New York, N. Y. 10021. This film depicts episodes in the life of Solomon Schechter, a scholar, teacher, and important figure in Conservative Judaism. It highlights his discovery of ancient Hebrew documents in Cairo. The script and acting are good. Recommended for high school audiences.

The Distorted Image: Stereotype and Caricature in American Popular Graphics, 1850 to 1922. Produced and distributed by the Anti-Defamation League of B'nai B'rith, 315 Lexington Avenue, New York, N. Y. 10014, 1973. This is a package which contains 60 slides, a cassette and a detailed discussion guide. The slides are cartoons and illustrations from large circulation magazines which reveal the extent and nature of stereotyping which has affected all minority groups in the United States. It concentrates on four ethnic groups in particular: the Chinese, Irish, Blacks and Jews. The presentation is designed for *advanced* high school courses. The discussion guide contains a suggested two-day lesson plan on the subject of stereotyping in general.

The Ghetto Pillow, a film produced by Albert Barry, 1960, 21 minutes, color. Distributed by Contemporary Films McGraw-Hill, 1221 Ave. of the Americas, New York, N. Y. 10020. This film gives a warm and vivid picture of ghetto life in eastern Europe. It is based on a series of water color paintings by Samuel Rothbort. It is very impressionistic but will nonetheless be suitable for mature high school students who are already familiar with the nature of the ghetto of East Europe.

The Golden Age of Second Avenue, a prize-winning film, produced and distributed by Arthur Cantor, Inc., 234 West 44th St., New York, N. Y. 10036, 1968. 67 minutes, color and black and white. A dramatic and delightful review of New York Jewish life and the Yiddish Theatre. Nostalgic and informative. Suitable for high school audiences. Contact the distributor for rental fee before ordering. Rates may be prohibitively high.

The Inheritance, a film produced by the Amalgamated Clothing Workers of America, 1964. 35 minutes, black and white. Distributed by the Anti-Defamation League of B'nai B'rith, 315 Lexington Ave., New York, N. Y. 10016, or regional ADL offices. This is an extremely effective film on the late nineteenth and early twentieth century migrations to the United States, using historic film footage and still photographs. It gives a balanced presentation of the social, economic, and cultural growth of America's immigrant communities. It does not dwell exclusively on the Jewish experience. There is strong emphasis on the trade union movement and on the garment industry. The film makes frequent use of labor terminology, with which students should be familiar before screening. This is an excellent film. Many teachers consider it the best of its kind ever produced. Highly recommended for high school students.

The Last Chapter, a film produced by Benjamin and Lawrence Rothman, 1965. 90 minutes, black and white. Distributed by Ben-Lar Productions, Inc., 22 East 17th St., New York, N. Y. 10003. This is a gripping documentary on the Polish-Jewish community before its destruction by the Nazis. It traces 1,000 years of history, using excellent documentary footage. The musical score is by Vladimir Heifetz, narration by Theodore Bikel. Highly recommended for high school audiences studying either Jewish life in eastern Europe or the Holocaust. Because of its length, it will probably require at least two class periods for screening.

Rabbinic Schools In America, a filmstrip, produced and distributed by the Audio-Visual Department, Bureau of Jewish Education, 590 N. Vermont Ave., Los Angeles, California 90004, 1957. 50 frames, black and white, includes teacher's guide. This filmstrip discusses the three major rabbinic seminaries in the United States, Reform, Conservative and Orthodox. It sheds light on principal variations within American Judaism. Suitable for junior and senior high school students.

This famous photograph, taken from German archives, shows Nazi soldiers rounding up "the enemy" in the Warsaw ghetto. The last survivors, almost unarmed, held off an armored Nazi division for many days in the heroic Battle of the Warsaw ghetto.

CHAPTER VII

THE ERA OF TWO WORLD WARS

*

IMPORTANT EVENTS

1904	*The Protocols of the Elders of Zion* is published in Russia (imported to the U.S. after World War I).
1914	Louis D. Brandeis becomes leader of the American Zionist Movement.
1917	The Balfour Declaration calls for a national home in Palestine for the Jewish people.
1924	The Johnson Act favors British and northern European immigrants, restricts the entry of eastern and southern Europeans.
1925	Resurrected Ku Klux Klan attains membership of four to five million.
1939-1945	Jewish communities of Europe are decimated in the Nazi Holocaust.
1947	The United Nations partitions Palestine into Jewish and Arab states.
1948	The State of Israel is proclaimed.

The Quota System

Until the outbreak of war in 1914, which interrupted the flow of immigrants to the United States, industrial expansion created an insatiable demand for labor, holding wide the door to continued immigration. With the cessation of hostilities, the flow resumed until nationalistic passions generated by the war, a growing fear of foreigners, and the longstanding opposition of organized labor finally led to a drastic reversal of the traditional open-door immigration policy.

The principal source of opposition was organized labor, which feared low-wage competition from alien workers.

Samuel Gompers, president of the American Federation of Labor and himself an immigrant Jew, led the movement. He was opposed by the majority of leaders in the Jewish community. In addition xenophobic and anti-Semitic factors accounted in part for the new attitude. Cries against violations of American "purity" were raised, and Americans began to read racist literature that preached the superiority of white eastern Europeans. Super patriots stigmatized foreigners as an alien element in American life, and viewed immigrants from eastern and southern Europe as carriers of the Bolshevik germ, rampant abroad. Many Americans blamed immigration for all their problems.

From 1882 to 1914 there were no serious restrictions on immigration. In 1917 an immigration act was passed over President Wilson's veto. It imposed a literacy test, which for Jews was not a serious restriction. Nearly all Jews were literate in Yiddish or Hebrew, which was sufficient. Furthermore, fugitives from religious persecution were exempt. A much more restrictive immigration act was signed into law by President Harding in 1921. It limited immigrants to an annual quota of three percent of a country's nationals residing in the United States in 1910. It also imposed a maximum of 357,000 in any one year. Earlier immigration had frequently exceeded a million per year. Jewish immigrants were reduced from 100,000 or more to 20,000 per year, since Jews came principally from countries with low quotas. In 1924 the Johnson Act halved the total, reduced the annual quota to two percent, and moved back the year for determining it to 1890. This was clearly to reduce quotas from eastern and southern Europe. The law favored the British and northern Europeans and succeeded not only in restricting Jewish immigration but in establishing a pattern which discriminated against all who were not western or northern Europeans. Only three countries, Great Britain, Germany, and Ireland, were allocated about seventy percent of the total quota of immigrants for the Eastern Hemisphere. In subsequent years changes were made in the immigration law, but the quota system was retained. It was only in 1965 that the Immigration and Nationality Act was amended to abolish the system of national preferences. A ceiling of 170,000 immigrants per year for the Eastern Hemisphere was set, with a maximum of 20,000 for any one country.

Jewish Identity

An outstanding feature of the Jewish community, as a whole, in the 1920's was its exodus from the urban slums in which the first generation of immigrants had settled. The prosperity of the war years and the decade which followed enabled many to move to newer middle-class areas of second settlement, where they tended to mix with more assimilated German Jews. Some of the German Jews, in turn, moved to areas of third settlement in either expensive urban districts or in the suburbs, foreshadowing a trend which was to become common after World War II.

Those who remained behind in the older neighborhoods tended to be the poorer, more religious Jews. Eastern European Orthodoxy consequently survived in its purest form in these ghetto areas. Kosher restaurants flourished and a variety of Jewish schools, Yiddish publications and Orthodox synagogues contributed to a viable Jewish life.

It was in the areas of second settlement, where most American Jews lived during the 1930's and 1940's, that cultural and religious patterns emerged which were to modify the future of American Jewish life. The most important was a drifting away from traditional religious practice by the overwhelming majority of the young. While they nominally remained Jews, they were either indifferent to or openly skeptical of Jewish ritual. Moreover, the means available to the various American Jewish communities to coerce the religious behavior of their members were minimal. In Europe, the state on occasion granted coercive powers to religious communities, including the Jewish community. In America separation of church and state precluded any such arrangement, with the result that each religious community was only a voluntary association to which the individual was free to adhere or not.

In America the Jewish community was further weakened in the eyes of some members because it shared such functions as marriage and divorce with the state. In eastern Europe such things had been the exclusive tasks of religious officials. Many American Jews, no longer bound by the restraints of an elaborate religious-legal code, which served to distinguish them from their gentile neighbors, dropped the traditional patterns of Jewish law, custom, and observance. Relieved at finding themselves in a land where they were not persecuted, they ceased to think of themselves as aliens in a foreign land and began to assimilate into the community around them.

Such attitudes seemed to foreshadow the demise of Judaism in America, yet that is not what happened. Though substantial numbers of Jews had moved away from their traditional religion, most maintained a strong desire to preserve their Jewish cultural identity and pass it on to their children. This is partly indicated by the very high rate of endogamous marriage among Jews and by the fact that in the 1920's and 1930's late-afternoon Jewish schools continued to grow. Even as Jewish families departed the areas of first settlement, they did not abandon the idea of Jewish education. Now congregational schools were established, which continued to attract large enrollments each year.

Educational and Social Mobility

Poverty was a constant companion of the immigrant Jewish working classes. Powerful unions helped improve their immediate conditions but the workers were determined that their children would not be laborers. Consequently Jewish children were kept in school until age fifteen or sixteen, long before compulsory attendance laws made that the norm. Jewish workers often refused to teach their trade to their sons and Jewish mothers sought employment in factories less frequently than did women of other immigrant groups. Thus the

Jewish child tended to receive better education and better care than other immigrant children, a fact reflected in lower juvenile delinquency and death rates among Jews than among many other groups.

A passion for education was characteristic of the Jewish immigrants who saw it as a way out of the slums. Within the span of one or two generations, most observable from 1920 to 1940, American Jews transformed themselves from a working-class to a middle-class community engaged in business, white-collar work, and the professions. During the same period of time Jews became one of the best educated segments of American society. For many, education represented a rational, calculated decision to leave the working class. But this too-simple explanation does not account for the inordinate propensity of young Jewish men to choose professions in which opportunities at first were few and prejudice against them strong, or the fact that parents regularly provided their daughters with an education far in excess of legal requirements, or why many third-generation Jews, reared in upper-middle-class homes, have abandoned the family business in favor of academic careers in the arts and sciences, the cultural professions such as journalism, literature, and publishing, or the traditional free professions of law and medicine. A more likely explanation is to be found in Jewish culture itself, which esteems education as a positive good and places a high value on learning for its own sake. This was part of the value system the immigrant brought with him, for throughout Jewish history generations of pious Jews had sustained the tradition of education in their perpetual study of the Torah. The religiosity of second and third generation American Jews may have been minimal but their zeal for study was not less than that of their ancestors. Education clearly led to social and economic mobility but the Jewish hunger for learning reflects far more than mere investment of time in school for a given return.

This passion for knowledge which the immigrants imparted to their children was to have consequences far beyond the

Jewish community itself, not the least of which is a remarkable record of achievement in various sciences, particularly in such subjects as mathematics, physics, and the biological, medical, and social sciences. This tradition of American Jewish scientific creativity was inaugurated by Albert Abraham Michelson. Born in Prussia in 1852, Michelson was brought to California as a child by his immigrant parents. He won a Presidential appointment to Annapolis, where he excelled in physics. After his graduation he began the researches that were to culminate in his measurement of the speed of light. In 1907 Michelson became the first American winner of the Nobel Prize in physics and the first of many American Jews who have been so honored. It is almost uncanny to read the biographies of American Jewish scientists and to note the large number who emerged from the very milieu described in this chapter. Backed by the self-sacrifice and encouragement of their immigrant parents, educated in the public schools, and with almost unparalleled access to competitive higher education, they have compiled one of the best arguments ever for free enterprise of the mind. Choosing names not quite at random, one notes that George Wald, a Harvard professor awarded the Nobel Prize in medicine in 1967 for his work on the biology of vision, was born in New York in 1906, the child of immigrants. His father was a garment worker. Jonas Salk, the discoverer of the first polio vaccine, was also the son of a garment worker. Albert B. Sabin, also the developer of a polio vaccine, was born in Poland in 1906 and brought to America at the age of fifteen. Simon Kuznets was born in Russia in 1901. He immigrated to America, studied economics at Columbia University, and was one of the first winners of the Nobel Prize in that subject for his invention of the concept of the Gross National Product. Selman Abraham Waksman, the discoverer of streptomycin, was the son of a weaver. He was born in Russia and immigrated to the United States where he studied microbiology. He was awarded the Nobel Prize in medicine in 1952.

The list of eminent American Jewish scientists could be

Albert Abraham Michelson became the first American winner of the Nobel Prize in physics and the first of many American Jews who have been so honored.

Selman Abraham Waksman, the discoverer of streptomycin, was awarded the Nobel Prize in medicine in 1952.

much longer. These examples suggest what the combination of respect for learning and unimpeded access to education has meant for American Jews and through them for mankind.

The upward occupational mobility of native-born Jews within the span of a few decades has paralleled their educational attainments. Jews have departed blue-collar occupations in far greater numbers than non-Jews. Their rise reflects favorably on the fluidity of class lines in America where the son of an immigrant tailor could enter the professions or attain a graduate degree.

Politics

The political behavior of American Jews forms an interesting contrast to their educational and occupational achievements. American Jewish voters are generally committed to liberal candidates and causes, no doubt reflecting a history which regularly denied them civil and political equality. Their political behavior seems to counter the assumption that wealth, education, and status make one inevitably a political conservative. American Jews are preponderantly middle class, highly educated, frequently found in professional, scientific, and entrepreneurial occupations, yet in their political attitudes they tend toward the liberal position as they have since their earliest days in America. They have usually voted for progressive candidates. An overwhelming majority of American Jews voted for Franklin D. Roosevelt and the New Deal which promised relief from the economic distress of the Depression. The New Deal, having demonstrated its willingness to legislate in economic and social matters, seemed to promise action to protect minorities against discrimination, a matter of particular concern to Jews in the 1930's. The fact that a number of Jews such as Felix Frankfurter, Sidney Hillman, and Benjamin V. Cohen were close to President Roosevelt may have helped convince them of the good intentions of the government toward Jews.

By the 1930's American Jews had generally committed themselves to the Democratic party, to which the progressive-liberal coalition had shifted. Since then they have consistently supported the Democratic ticket in national elections. In the 1970's there are some indications that Jewish voters are increasingly attracted to the Republican party and that their political preferences much more nearly resemble those of their non-Jewish counterparts similarly situated in income, occupation, and education.

Anti-Semitism

In the twentieth century anti-Semitism in America became very significant. In the 1890's farmers, faced by mounting economic difficulties, were increasingly attracted to the free-silver proposals of the Populists. The movement never officially espoused a program of anti-Semitism, but it did much to create the image of a money trust conspiring against the poor. Many farmers and unemployed workers, facing foreclosure, found it comforting to blame their problems on the "money power," which was variously described as the aloof, aristocratic English financier or the even more "sinister" foreign Jewish banker, who formed part of an "international conspiracy." Jews have frequently been victims of this type of scapegoating. The fact that a few banking houses in Europe were Jewish-owned may have led to the myth that Jews controlled the great fortunes of the world.

After the turn of the century, with the defeat of Populism, demagogues like Tom Watson of Georgia preached a policy of hatred. Watson first attacked the Blacks, then the Catholics, and finally the Jews. His inflammatory preaching contributed to the lynching in 1915 of Leo Frank, a Jew falsely accused of murder, partly because he was a northern Jew in a Southern town.

In 1891 a magazine claimed that Jews had been absent from the armed forces during the Civil War. In 1908 a New York City police commissioner charged that a disproportionate number of New York's criminals were immigrant Russian Jews. He retracted the story when challenged by the newly formed American Jewish Committee. But anti-Semitism

Help Wanted Women—Agencies

NATIONAL

EMPOYMENT EXCHANGE
30 Church St.,- 7th Floor
Hudson Terminal Building

"Specializing in Outstanding Personnel"

INTERVIEWS
Mon.-Fri., 9-2; Sat.. 9-12
appointment for those
now employed

Radio City—42nd St. Area

MULTIg.; kn. mineog.-address, Chr $23
STENO, charge small office, to 27 years, Christian, 5 day week...$20
STENO-Recept; to 26, nice appear. $20
DICT. Op, 2 yr. exp, pleasant off..$20
ASST. Bkpr., Mt. Vernon, Chr ...$20
RECEP-Steno, monitor bd., Chr ..$20
STENO, knowl. bkpg, Chr $18-20
STENO; will teach switchbd, Chr .$18
TYPIST-Clk, bright begin.. consid.$70
STENO, knowl. bkpg;beg. cons Prot $17

Lower Manhattan Area

F. C. BKPr, 28-32, knowledge typing, West Side, Chr, 5 day week....$30
SPANish-English Stenos........$25-30
STENO, 23-27, engineering, small office, rapid, Christian, future....$25
LEGAL Steno, 1 mo., Chr 5 day..$25
MONITor Board - Receptionist -Typist, steno help., 21-25, attrac., Chr .$25
SWITCHboard-Typist-Receptionist, 24-28 yrs., single, Chr ....to $25
EDIPHone-Swbd., to 30 yrs., Chr .$23
STENO, recent shipping expr.....$23
ASST. Bkpr-Typist, 20-22 yrs, accounting future, Christian $20-23
COMPTom, yng, exp;future Chr St. $90
STENO, 20-25, insurance, Chr $22
JR. SECys-Stenos, excellent firms, bright begin. or expd., Chr ..$18-21
STENO, statemt. typ; yng, 5d; Prot $20
STENO, expd. monitor board, Chr. .$20
STENO, to 23, insur. help., Chr. .$20
STENO, expd. biller, Christian ...$20
EDIPHone, to 28, exp, Catholic ..$20
EDIPHone Operators, several openings, leading firms, Christian.......$20

This classified advertisement illustrates one type of prejudice Jews were faced with in America. Forty out of forty-seven jobs advertised specify "Christian."

continued to spread. "Scientific" anti-Semitism, which attempted to "prove" that Jews were biologically inferior, spread from Germany to America.

Immediately following World War I, immigration from Europe resumed, only to decline drastically with the immigration laws of the early 1920's which were inspired, at least in part, by the anti-Semitism of the preceding two decades. Millions of Jews, having suffered the dislocations of war, might have immigrated to America but for the restrictive legislation which was designed to stop them.

The Ku Klux Klan reappeared with a policy of native white Protestant supremacy. It condemned Blacks, Jews, Catholics and the foreign-born. By 1925 it had attracted four to five million members as postwar dislocations and frustrations and a shrewd organizational campaign swelled its ranks. The Klan entered politics and made gains in many regions of the country. It labeled the Jew "an unblendable element," burned fiery crosses in front of synagogues, and broke the store windows of Jewish merchants. It declined in power at the end of the 1920's with the conviction of Klan leaders who had enriched themselves from Klan funds and with the passage in some states of laws banning secret meetings.

In Russia, in 1904, a pamphlet entitled "The Protocols of the Elders of Zion," was published. It was a complete and fantastic forgery, purporting to be the minutes of a secret meeting of Jewish leaders in Prague who were plotting to overthrow the world. The book was a clumsy fabrication, yet many Europeans accepted it and when it appeared in the United States after World War I a surprisingly large audience was also ready to believe it. Henry Ford helped publicize the falsehood by publishing the slanders in his weekly paper, *The Dearborn Independent*. Ford even attacked specific Jews until 1926, when Aaron Sapiro, a prominent Jewish lawyer, sued him for a million dollars. The trial was never finished because Ford publicly apologized to Sapiro and to the Jewish people as a whole. (He had noted a decline in Ford sales as a boycott began to take effect.)

This effectively ended the matter in America, but Ford's name continued to lend credence to the forgery abroad. It is significant that this case of anti-Semitism was sponsored by a private citizen, not the government. Anti-Semitism has rarely, if ever, received governmental sanction in this country as it has in Europe. It is this immensely important fact which distinguishes anti-Semitism in America from the classical, government-sponsored attacks in Europe. Nonetheless, it can be as dangerous when directed by private groups as when it is public policy. Even in private hands it has led to serious discrimination in housing, jobs, education and social clubs.

In 1929 the Great Depression struck. People out of work were desperate and vulnerable to racist agitation. Irrational charges were made that Jewish bankers, controlling world finance, had rigged the depression in a conspiracy against Christendom. *Fortune* published the results of a survey in February, 1936, which proved that Jews played, at best, a minimal role in national and international banking, but the lie persisted. Jews were attacked as radicals, international bankers, Reds and warmongers. Anti-Semites ridiculed the New Deal as a Jewish concoction. They called it the "Jew Deal" and referred to "President Rosenfeld." Their hatred stemmed, in some measure, from the fact that among President Franklin D. Roosevelt's advisers were many capable Jews. Union leaders David Dubinsky and Sydney Hillman, Supreme Court Justice Felix Frankfurter, legal counselor Samuel Rosenman, and Secretary of the Treasury Henry Morgenthau, Jr. were all Jews who were assisting the administration.

Later in the 1930's, when to the still lingering effects of the Depression, were added the tensions arising from the deteriorating international situation, these sentiments began to assume an even darker hue. An attempt was made to export Nazism to the United States. Fascist organizations sprang up, blaming the woes of the world on the Jews. Secret agents coached native *fuehrers* in the technique of anti-Semitic propaganda, which intensified hatred of Jews. Father Charles

E. Coughlin, the Detroit "radio priest," revived the old idea that Jews were joined in a conspiracy to take over the world. His weekly radio program reached millions and his blatantly anti-Jewish publication, *Social Justice,* was peddled on the busiest streets of America.*

What is most remarkable about all such activity was its marginality to the mainstream of American political life and its failure to capture or even substantially influence established American political institutions and habits. Politicians and legislators paid no heed to the anti-Semitic groups of the twenties and thirties. As the dangers of Nazism became more apparent and its link to many of these groups was revealed, they died out. It was the spirit and traditions of America which really smothered the Nazi spark. America, as a whole, never swallowed the anti-Jewish bait proffered by the hate-mongers. With few exceptions, leaders in all aspects of American life turned their backs on anti-Semitism and many even joined the campaign against it.

Zionism

These domestic achievements and preoccupations absorbed most but not all of the energies of American Jews, who became increasingly alarmed over the fate of their coreligionists in Europe, as fascism grew during the 1930's. Their concerns, however, were not entirely without precedent, for even in the nineteenth century, American Jews had frequently voiced anxiety over the well-being of Jews in other lands. By the end of that century, with eastern European Jewry repeatedly subjected to the bloody pogroms of the Czar and with no relief in sight for the fearful poverty in which many Jews lived, the conviction began to grow among an increasing number of Jews that the solution to the "Jewish problem" lay in ending the condition of exile in which Jews had lived for centuries.

*Coughlin never enjoyed the support of the Catholic hierarchy and was silenced by the Church in May, 1942 for his increasingly pro-Fascist position.

A Jewish state had, of course, existed in Palestine in antiquity for whose restoration Jews had never ceased to pray. The modern Zionist movement—as the proposal for the return of the Jewish people to Zion (Palestine) has come to be known—may be said to have originated in 1896, when Theodore Herzl, an assimilated Viennese journalist, summoned the first Zionist congress, in Basle, Switzerland. Its aim was "the establishment for the Jewish people of a publicly and legally assured home in Palestine." In little more than half a century this aim was to be realized.

In America, Zionism drew its strength from the membership of hundreds of Orthodox and Conservative congregations, from the eastern European immigrants and their children. It numbered among its masses, storekeepers and peddlers, sweatshop and factory workers, whose memories of persecution and poverty in the old world were still vivid. It included those who felt an instinctive sympathy for the Zionist ideal of a restored Jewish homeland which would serve as a haven, if not for themselves, then for their fellow Jews living abroad.

Opponents were generally Reform Jews of German extraction, the children and grandchildren of the "Forty-Eighters." They had achieved affluence and status in America and found the Zionist thesis that Jews were insecure and vulnerable everywhere, including the United States, difficult to accept. They rejected the Zionist idea, for a Jewish state raised in their minds the question of dual nationality and divided allegiance, which, they feared, could erode the security they felt in America. But in the next few decades even their attitude gradually changed to one of support, as the realities of war, the Nazi Holocaust, and the imminent reestablishment of the Jewish state became obvious. The change may also have been due in part to a shift by the Reform movement in the late 1930's to a somewhat more traditional Jewish position.

With the outbreak of World War I, membership in the fledgling Zionist Organization in the United States soared. A major factor in its growth was the emergence of Louis D.

Louis Dembitz Brandeis (1856-1941), Justice of the Supreme Court, once said: "American ideals have been Jewish ideals for twenty centuries."

Brandeis as the leader of American Zionism. He was the most prestigious national figure the cause had yet attracted. While some American Jews could not reconcile Zionism with loyalty to America, Brandeis succinctly dealt with the problem by explaining that "to be good Americans, we must be better Jews, and to be better Jews we must become Zionists." Regarding the spectre of dual allegiance, he said simply, "Multiple loyalties are objectionable only if they are inconsistent."

The movement gained further strength in 1917 when Woodrow Wilson supported Great Britain's Balfour Declaration which declared: "His Majesty's Government view with favour the establishment in Palestine of a national home for the Jewish people. . . ." The Declaration was also endorsed by the United States Congress. In the eyes of American Jews, Zionism had become a legitimate endeavor. It now had the sanction of their own government.

The Holocaust

The reëstablishment of a Jewish homeland in Palestine was not, of course, the only international concern of American Jewry. Germany in the 1930's became a hell on earth for the Jewish people as Hitler unleashed an unprecedented anti-Jewish hysteria. In 1933 books by Jewish writers were burned. Jews were deprived of their citizenship and professions. They were forced to wear the yellow badge with the Star of David that their ancestors had been forced to wear. Synagogues were burned in hundreds of cities and towns. As the Nazi terror spread over much of Europe, millions of Jews were sent to concentration camps. Six million Jews were ultimately killed by the Germans, four million of them systematically and diabolically killed in specially built extermination camps.

Rumors of the Nazi horror trickled out of Germany during the war. The world simply could not grasp the meaning of such evil. General Eisenhower invited a delegation of editors and Congressmen to see the evidence first hand. The great European centers of Jewish scholarship and learning were gone. Because of the dreadful losses in Europe, by the end of World War II over half of the Jews remaining in the world lived in the United States.

In the years preceding the outbreak of the war, when America might have offered a haven to millions, the Johnson Act of 1924 permitted only a few to enter. In 1939 about 43,000 Jews managed to reach America and as late as 1941 the figure came to about 23,000. After that year few could escape from Europe. In 1944 the number of Jews who managed to reach the United States fell to the pitiful figure of 2,400. America's restrictive immigration laws made it impossible for large numbers of Jews to come to this nation when escape was relatively easy.

The limited number of refugees who did reach America during these years, primarily from the well-to-do classes with money necessary for escape, included a high percentage of professors, scientists, and intellectuals. Many were men and women of national and international reputation. Best-known among them was Albert Einstein.

The United States did little to help the victims of Nazi Germany. Rescue efforts in the 1930's were tragically ineffective. As early as 1934 the League of Nations had appointed a commission for the protection of Jewish and non-Jewish refugees but it was a failure, since not even the democracies were willing to relax their restrictive immigration laws. A number of heads of state expressed shock and dismay, but the strongest "action" managed by any was that of President Roosevelt when he recalled the American Ambassador from Berlin in the late 1930's. Roosevelt also summoned a conference of thirty nations which met in Evian, France, in 1938, to consider the situation. Except for lofty sentiments and profound regrets, it too did nothing.

In April, 1942, a conference of American and British delegates met in Bermuda to consider rescue measures but it did no more than the earlier Evian Conference. In January, 1944, Roosevelt appointed a War Refugee Board to try to save the victims of Hitler. It worked with underground anti-Nazi groups in various countries and had some success in the

Balkan states and in France. However, it was much too little and much too late to be significant. It only served to show the world what might have been accomplished had the democracies acted sooner.

The book, *While Six Million Died,* by Arthur Morse, recounts in detail how the United States did nearly nothing to aid victims of Nazi atrocities. In fact, their plight was deliberately ignored. Ships carrying refugees from Germany were turned away from American shores and returned to the European holocaust! The United States government even refused to save groups of several thousand children. The refusal of the western nations to accept Jewish refugees only strengthened the determination of Zionists the world over to reëstablish a homeland in Palestine, which would provide a haven for persecuted Jews from any land.

The State of Israel

After World War II, when the full dimensions of the Nazi destruction were revealed, and the culpability of the Western nations in not accepting Jewish refugees was evident, the world community of nations became more receptive to Zionist aspirations. In the United States, the support of the general public for a Jewish state was widespread. Prominent Christian leaders, state legislatures, and governors, as well as many Jews, endorsed the Zionist program. In 1944 the nominating conventions of the two major political parties included pro-Zionist planks in their platforms, and both houses of Congress adopted pro-Zionist resolutions.

On November 29, 1947, the General Assembly of the United Nations partitioned Palestine into a Jewish state and an Arab state. On May 14, 1948, Britain gave up her mandate under which she had administered the area since the end of World War I. On the same day the State of Israel was proclaimed with Chaim Weizmann as president and David Ben-Gurion as prime minister. President Truman recognized the new nation immediately.

Immediately after the British withdrew, Israel became in-

The present State of Israel was created on May 14, 1948. President Harry Truman immediately announced that the United States would accord recognition to the new State. The above picture depicts an early agricultural settlement at Yokneam.

This Government has been informed that a Jewish state has been proclaimed in Palestine, and recognition has been requested by the provisional Government thereof.

The United States recognizes the provisional government as the de facto authority of the new ~~Jewish state~~ State of Israel.

Harry Truman

Approved, May 14. 1948.

The draft statement, signed and approved by President Truman, recognizing the provisional government of the new State of Israel.

volved in a war with her Arab neighbors who were bent on the destruction of the new state. War has erupted repeatedly since that time.

Though Israel receives the wholehearted financial and political support of most of America's Jews, this rarely raises in their own minds any question of divided loyalties. America claims their full allegiance, but their pride in being Jewish has been enhanced by the achievements, not to speak of the sheer survival, of Israel. Israel has provided a home for hundreds of thousands of Jewish refugees, has maintained a democratic political system amid the largely despotic and one-party political systems of the Middle East, and has built up in a few short years a flourishing network of schools, universities, scientific institutes, and cultural facilities. Contrary to the fears that were occasionally heard during the early years of the Zionist movement, the existence of the State of Israel has enhanced the security of American Jews. By not migrating to Israel in substantial numbers, American Jews have indicated that America is their home.

TO THE TEACHER:

This chapter opens with an account of the various forces which opposed free immigration to the United States. Organized labor, epitomized by Samuel Gompers, an immigrant Jew, was a prime opponent, though Gomper's view was shared by few in the Jewish community. Teachers could use this fact in at least two ways. It suggests that occupation and environment are often more important in influencing behavior than ethnic or religious origin, and it focuses directly on labor's traditional fear of cheap, foreign competition. But other forces also opposed free immigration. The xenophobic and anti-Semitic antipathies generated by the Red scare were also important. The legislation which curbed immigration from eastern and southern Europe was by no means limited to Jews, who were affected along with numerous other ethnic minorities.

The sociological and demographic features of the maturing

Jewish community illuminate the process of urbanization and the shifting population patterns which characterized the second- and third-generation children of the immigrants who moved from the teeming neighborhoods in which their parents originally settled to areas of second settlement and finally to the suburbs. As they left, Blacks and other ethnic groups moved into the neighborhoods abandoned by the Jews. The process is intrinsic to an understanding of twentieth century urban America. The teacher should have a clear understanding of the words "ghetto" and "slum" which, though used interchangeably, are quite distinct in meaning. A "slum" is a run-down area, while a "ghetto" is an area which may or may not be a slum, but which is composed of an ethnically homogeneous people. In Europe the ghetto referred to the section of a city to which Jews were confined.

Equally important for study in the social studies class is the desire of Jews to preserve their identity, a phenomenon which reflects such concepts as ethnic pride and ethnic survival. In Europe, Jews had been kept distinct and apart from the general population. In America the opposite was true, and Jews faced the danger of assimilation within the dominant society. Yet they stubbornly resisted the loss of ethnic identity by marrying endogamously and by educating their children as Jews. Endogamous marriage raises the subject of interracial and interreligious marriage. Students should be encouraged to consider the sociological implications of this subject.

The passion for education which characterized the eastern European immigrants, should be treated as a study in values. Jews value education. The Jewish scientists, scholars, musicians, and leaders in various fields who are mentioned in this chapter are products of that value system.

The tendency of Jews to support liberal political candidates provides an intriguing contrast with the political behavior of other ethnic groups, though Jews were not alone in flocking to the Democratic party during the New Deal era. The New Deal took over the work of many Jewish communal agencies. Discussion of the New Deal offers teachers an excellent opportunity to deal with the relationship between private and public sources of welfare in the United States.

Anti-Semitism between the Civil War and World War I is a little-known aspect of American history. The stereotype generated by the Populists of the "money power" might prove useful to teachers in illustrating the frustrations of poor farmers and unemployed workers who found it comforting to "project" their difficulties onto rich bankers, English financiers, and Jews. The xenophobia which gripped America in the aftermath of World War I constitutes an unpleasant but important bit of American social history, as does the rise of the Ku Klux Klan in the twenties, which was not only anti-Negro, but anti-Catholic, anti-Jewish, and anti-immigrant, as well. Study of the Protocols of the Elders of Zion provides an intriguing lesson in anti-Semitism and xenophobia as well as in the technique of propaganda. Despite Henry Ford's dissemination of the Protocols, the striking feature of this incident, which must be stressed above all else, is that anti-Semitism in America, at least in its more virulent forms, was confined to the lunatic fringe. It never had the support of government, as it did in many European nations.

The establishment of the State of Israel, which posed for some American Jews the question of dual nationality and divided allegiance, might generate a provocative classroom discussion on the nature of citizenship, nationality, loyalty, and patriotism. Brandeis' assertion that "multiple loyalties are objectionable only if they are inconsistent" should be discussed at this point. What bearing does it have on the role of hyphenated (i.e., Jewish-Americans, Irish-Americans) groups in our society? What does it say about group loyalties in general?

Zionism might be compared to the efforts of Marcus Garvey, who sponsored a return-to-Africa movement for Black Americans at roughly the same time that Zionism was gaining ground. Zionism attracted European Jewish immigrants to Palestine, while Garvey's appeal was addressed to native-born American Negroes. Zionism might also be contrasted to the work of the American Colonization Society which settled free Blacks in the State of Liberia.

Another topic which demands attention is the Nazi Holocaust. Michael B. Kane in his 1969 study, *Minorities in Textbooks,*[1] found that nearly thirty percent of the textbooks in general use in social studies classes omitted reference to this topic and nearly fifty percent gave it inadequate coverage. More recently Saul Friedman found a similar situation in college textbooks,[2] as did Henry Friedlander.[3] Postwar and contemporary Jewish attitudes have been powerfully influenced by the Holocaust and by the haunting suspicion that the United States and the Western nations did not do all that they might have done to save the intended victims of the Nazi genocide or even to accommodate the refugees who managed to escape the Nazi terror. This raises a host of questions for the social studies classroom. To what extent should a people protest against an indifferent government? To what extent was the apathy and indifference of the United States responsible for the death of millions? Could the same thing happen today? Is today's youth more prone to demonstrate for what it considers right? What accounts for the difference?

1. Michael B. Kane, *Minorities in Textbooks,* Quadrangle Books, 1969, p. 75.
2. Saul Friedman, *Jewish Frontier,* July, 1972.
3. Henry Friedlander, *On the Holocaust,* Anti-Defamation League of B'nai B'rith, 1973.

DISCUSSION QUESTIONS AND STUDENT ACTIVITIES

1. Trace the history of immigration laws in the United States. What is the law at this time?
2. Conduct a debate. Resolved: Free and unlimited immigration to the United States is desirable.
3. Have students prepare a family tree in which they trace their ancestry back at least as far as is necessary to show ancestors born outside the United States. Display them in class; discuss any diversity of immigrant backgrounds. A variation would be to have students write a history of either set of grandparents, based on personal interviews with them, with parents or with other relatives. Use of family documents as sources should be encouraged. Try to answer such questions as where grandparents or great-grandparents came from, how they met, why they came to America (if appropriate), occupations, political views, etc.
4. What accounts for Jewish survival after centuries of severe and consistent persecution in Europe? How does acceptance threaten Jews in America today? Discuss and defend your answers.
5. Report on the history of the Jewish *Kehillah* in New York City. Why was it doomed to fail? For source material consult Arthur Goren, *New York Jews in Pursuit of Community: The Kehilla Experiment, 1908-1922* (Columbia University Press, New York, 1970).
6. Prepare a photographic story of a slum, together with appropriate captions which will make it clear to the reader what life is like in a slum. This might be done with snap shots mounted for display, or as a movie or slide show with tape recorded narration, and live sound effects. How does a slum differ from an ethnically homogeneous "ghetto"? Discuss the Jewish ghettos in Europe and compare them with ghettos of poor minority groups today.
7. Report on Jonas Salk and his discovery of a polio vaccine. Describe his career in terms of the eastern European

Jewish immigration. Similar reports might be prepared for any of the successful scientists mentioned in this chapter. Try to indicate how their Jewish heritage and values influenced their lives.

8. Do a research report on voting patterns among American Jews. Determine how the Jewish population voted in the last Presidential election. Do Jews vote alike? Can one speak of a "Jewish" vote?
9. Identify some problem concerning prejudice, discrimination or anti-Semitism in your community. Phone or write the nearest office of the Anti-Defamation League of B'nai B'rith. Follow through for results and a solution to the problem. Write up the experience.
10. Write a research report on the lynching of Leo Frank, in 1915, a rare case of a Jew being lynched in the United States.
11. Prepare a report on the renewed Ku Klux Klan of the 1920's. What role did anti-Semitism play in its program? Account for its phenomenal rise and sudden decline at the end of the twenties. What is its status today?
12. In the periodicals section of a large library try to locate copies of Henry Ford's *Dearborn Independent* for the dates, May 22, through October 2, 1920. Find the series of anti-Semitic articles called "The International Jew," which were based on the forged "Protocols of the Elders of Zion." Comment on them as an example of hate propaganda.
13. If measured in terms of prejudice, anti-Semitism could be considered fairly common in the U.S. If measured in terms of actual discrimination, it is probably minimal. Discuss these differences in defining anti-Semitism. What predictions can you make about anti-Semitism in the future?
14. Write a report about anti-Semitism in the United States since 1945, its causes, its cures, its significance today. How can it be combatted?
15. Write a research paper comparing Zionism to Marcus

Garvey's return-to-Africa movement for American Blacks and the efforts of the American Colonization Society to settle Blacks in Liberia. Compare the success or failure of these movements.

16. Discuss Louis Brandeis' philosophy that "multiple loyalties are objectionable only if they are inconsistent." Make a list of the varying loyalties you have, such as school, family, church, government, etc. What conflicts exist? How do you deal with them?

17. Report on the Nazi-inspired hate organizations which sprouted in the United States in the 1930's. (Examples: the German-American Bund, The Silver Shirts, the Order of '72, etc.) Also report on Detroit's radio-priest, Father Charles E. Coughlin.

18. In what ways did the Nazi Holocaust resemble the Spanish Inquisition? In what ways did it differ? Can you account for the similarities and differences?

19. Obtain a class set of *Night* by Elie Wiesel. Read and discuss the personal experiences of the author in Nazi concentration camps. Relate the book to American history by discussing or writing about the following topics:
    - How did the U.S. combat Nazi atrocities in the fight against Germany?
    - What else could the U.S. have done to combat Nazi atrocities?
    - Why did the U.S. refuse to help the victims of Nazi persecutions?
    - What moral obligations did our nation neglect when it refused to revise immigration laws and even turned away Jewish refugees?
    - How many victims of Nazi persecution were relatives of American Jews?
    - Where in the world today are war crimes being committed? What is the U.S. doing about them?

20. Report on the Evian Conference in 1938, the Bermuda Conference in 1942 and the Oswego Plan in 1944. How

could the words of John Greenleaf Whittier be used to describe these efforts?

"For all sad words of tongue or pen
The saddest are these: 'It might have been!' "

21. Compare U.S. policy toward German anti-Semitism during World War II with what you think U.S. policy toward Soviet anti-Semitism should be today.
22. Have students discuss with Jewish acquaintances their attitudes about Israel. Would they like to live there, to visit there, to give financial assistance to Israel? Why? Have them report their findings to the class.
23. Write to the Jewish Agency, Department of Education and Culture (see appendix) for information on its work in the Zionist movement and about Israel today. Also write or visit the Israeli Consulate nearest you, or visit a travel agency for brochures, posters or information about Israel. Report on major similarities and differences between it and the United States in government, economic system or social life. What is Israel's attitude toward immigration from the United States?
24. Read and report on *Exodus* by Leon Uris or *The Source* by James Michener.

BIBLIOGRAPHY

Epstein, Benjamin R., and Forster, Arnold, *Some of My Best Friends* (Farrar, Straus and Cudahy, New York, 1962). Analyzes patterns of anti-Semitism in the United States in the early 1960's, particularly in social life, housing, higher education, and employment. Benjamin Epstein is the national director of the Anti-Defamation League of B'nai B'rith. Arnold Forster is the League's general counsel and director of its civil rights division. Suitable for teachers and high school students.

Finklestein, Milton, Sandifer, Hon. Jawn A., and Wright, Elfreda S., *Minorities, U.S.A.* (Globe Book Company, New York, 1971). This is intended as a text for high school courses in ethnic studies and for use as a resource in integrating ethnic materials into the American history curriculum. A number of minority groups are included. Unit 6 deals with "Jewish Americans." The second half is a good summary of anti-Semitism in America. Recommended for junior and senior high school students.

Handlin, Oscar, *Adventures in Freedom: Three Hundred Years of Jewish Life in America* (McGraw-Hill, New York, 1954). Chapter 8 is an excellent discussion of anti-Semitism from 1890 to 1941. Chapter 9 covers the Jewish community from 1920 to 1954. Chapter 10 covers the American Jewish community from 1920 to 1954. Recommended for teachers and capable high school students.

Learsi, Rufus, *The Jews in America: A History* (Ktav, New York, 1972). Chapter 30 is a good account of the anti-Semitism which prevailed in this country in the twenties and thirties. Chapters 17 and 18 deal with World War I and the ensuing peace. Chapters 20 and 22 deal with world Jewry and World War II, with strong emphasis on Zionism and the events leading to the establishment of the State of Israel in 1948. Suitable for teachers and capable high school students.

Levinger, Lee J., *A History of the Jews of the United States* (Union of American Hebrew Congregations, New York, 1961). Chapter 22 parallels much of the material in this unit. It is particularly strong on anti-Semitism, the new immigration laws, the effects of the Depression, and the Nazi influence in America. Recommended for junior and senior high school students.

Morse, Arthur, *While Six Million Died: A Chronicle of American Apathy* (Ace Publishing Corporation, New York, 1967). A well-documented narrative about the indifference of the United States government to the fate of the European Jews before and during World War II. Clearly illustrates that "no man is an island," and shows the need for continuing social responsibility. Recommended for teachers and capable high school students.

Peare, Catherine O., *The Louis D. Brandeis Story* (Cromwell, New York, 1970). A biography of Louis D. Brandeis, depicting his role as lawyer, Supreme Court justice, champion of labor, and Zionist leader. The story is told with warmth and affection. Recommended for junior high school students.

Sherman, C. Bezalel, *The Jew Within American Society: A Study in Ethnic Individuality* (Wayne State University Press, Detroit, 1961, also in paperback). An important book which analyzes the relationship of minorities to the dominant society in America and treats the Jews as a unique ethnic group. This theme is developed throughout the book, particularly in Chapter 6. Mr. Sherman includes excellent demographic, economic, social, and cultural data to support his theories. Chapter 8 is a good summary of the achievement of the eastern European Jewish immigrants. Chapter 9 deals with the economic mobility of the American Jew. Recommended for teachers and superior high school students.

St. John, Robert, *Jews, Justice and Judaism* (Doubleday, New

York, 1969). Chapter 18 includes among other things, a good discussion of "The Protocols of the Elders of Zion." Chapter 21 includes good sketches of Albert Einstein and Louis Brandeis. Recommended for teachers and high school students.

Wiesel, Elie, *Night* (Hill and Wang, N. Y., 1960). The personal experiences of the writer in Nazi concentration camps. Realistic horror but not too extreme for young students. Short and very readable. For mature junior high and all senior high readers.

Wischnitzer, Mark, *To Dwell in Safety* (Jewish Publication Society, Philadelphia, 1949). The story of Jewish migrations throughout the world since 1800. The last three chapters deal with Jewish migration after 1933. Chapter 6 is particularly good on migration during the Nazi era. Suitable for teachers and capable high school students.

AUDIO-VISUAL MATERIALS

Act of Faith, a film produced by the N. Y. Board of Rabbis in cooperation with CBS, 1961. 30 minutes, black and white. Available from the Anti-Defamation League of B'nai B'rith, 315 Lexington Avenue, New York, N. Y. 10016. Tells the dramatic story of the heroic Danish resistance movement against Hitler which succeeded in rescuing the Jews of Denmark. It is a firsthand account of the role played by the Danish people in saving their Jewish countrymen from Nazi extermination. Recommended for junior and senior high school audiences.

Albert Einstein, a filmstrip produced and directed by the Jewish Education Committee of New York, 426 West 58th Street, New York, N. Y. 10019, 1956. 47 frames, color. This is a prize-winning biographical filmstrip depicting Einstein's role as a leader in the world, within the Jewish community, and in the world of science. An excellent production. Highly recommended for high school audiences.

An American Girl, a film produced by Dynamic Films, 1958. 30 minutes, black and white. Available from the Anti-Defamation League of B'nai B'rith, 315 Lexington Avenue, New York, N. Y. 10016. This film about anti-Semitism and irrational prejudice is based on an actual incident that occurred in the 1950's. It tells the story of an American teenager who is mistakenly believed to be Jewish by her friends and neighbors. Recommended for junior and senior high school audiences.

The Anatomy of Nazism, a filmstrip produced by and available from the Anti-Defamation League of B'nai B'rith, 315 Lexington Avenue, New York, N. Y. 10016, 1962. 55 frames in length, color, and captioned. An historic presentation of the social, cultural, economic and political workings of Fascism in Hitler's Germany reflecting the general threat to democracy of all forms of totalitarianism. Suitable for junior and senior high school audiences.

Gentleman's Agreement, a feature film produced by 20th Century-Fox, starring Gregory Peck, Dorothy McGuire, John Garfield, and Celeste Holm, 1947, 118 minutes, black and white. Distributed by Audio/Brandon, 34 MacQuesten Parkway, So., Mount Vernon, N. Y. 10550 (or regional offices). This is the screen version of Laura Hobson's best-selling novel about a crusading journalist who poses as a Jew to expose the evils of anti-Semitism in American society. It is a good example of the use of an entertaining feature film for educational purposes. Because of its length, it will require several class periods for screening. Suitable for high school audiences.

Jewish Legends and Tales, a film produced by the Anti-Defamation League of B'nai B'rith in cooperation with the Archdiocese of New York, 1969. 30 minutes, black and white. Available from the Anti-Defamation League of B'nai B'rith, 315 Lexington Avenue, New York, N. Y. 10016. The noted novelist, Elie Wiesel, recounts tales and legends from the Midrash* through the stories which emerged during the Holocaust and explains their relevance today. He says "It is the same story that is being told over and over. What changes is the setting. What changes is the teller, not the tale." Mr. Wiesel talks of his own experiences in the Nazi Holocaust. Recommended for junior and senior high school audiences.

Lawyer From Boston, a kinescope film of the NBC-TV Religious Hour Program, "Frontiers of Faith", produced by the Jewish Theological Seminary of America in cooperation with the National Broadcasting Company, 1956. 30 minutes, black and white. Distributed by the National Academy for Adult Jewish Studies of the United Synagogue of America, 218 E. 70th Street, New York, N. Y. 10021. This film presents significant aspects in the life of Louis D. Brandeis. It is interesting, well-acted, and suitable for high school students studying American Zionism or labor relations in the United States.

Let My People Go, a documentary film produced by David L. Wolper Productions, 1965. 55 minutes, black and white. Distributed by the Jam Handy Organization, 2821 East Grand Boulevard, Detroit, Michigan, 48211. This film tells the story of the Jewish people's quest for a homeland, culminating in the birth of the State of Israel. Makes excellent use of documentary footage, including some captured German war films. Highly recommended for high school students studying either Zionism or the Nazi Holocaust.

Louis D. Brandeis: Giant of Justice and Champion of Zionism, a filmstrip produced by Samuel Grand, 1966. 42 frames, color, includes 2 detailed guides and scripts. Distributed by the Publications Department, Jewish Agency, 515 Park Avenue, New York, N. Y. 10022. This is an informative filmstrip about Louis D. Brandeis and his role as a leader

*Midrash. exposition; Talmudic literature consisting of wise sayings, tales, maxims and sermons which explain the Biblical text.

of American and world Jewry. The script is pedestrian and overwritten, but the production is useful for junior and senior high school groups.

Memorandum, a film produced by the National Film Board of Canada, 1966. 58 minutes, black and white. Distributed by the Anti-Defamation League of B'nai B'rith, 315 Lexington Avenue, New York, N. Y. 10016 and regional ADL offices. This outstanding film was produced to commemorate the 20th anniversary of the liberation of the Nazi death camps. A group of survivors return to one of the camps, Bergen-Belsen. Today's Germany is contrasted with the Germany of the Holocaust. This is a sensitive film which deals with the question of responsibility. Highly recommended for high school audiences, but students unaware of the Holocaust should be adequately prepared before screening.

A Nation of Immigrants, produced by Wolper Associates, Inc., 1961. 52 minutes, black and white. Distributed by the Anti-Defamation League of B'nai B'rith, 315 Lexington Avenue, New York, N. Y. 10016, and regional ADL offices. Based on the late President John F. Kennedy's book of the same title, this superb documentary traces the successive waves of immigration to the United States. Uses rare prints, early photographs, and archive film footage. Includes sequences depicting the hate-mongering America Firsters and Father Coughlin, who campaigned for restrictive immigration quotas. Narrated by Richard Basehart. Recommended for high school audiences.

Night and Fog, a Cocinor film presentation, 1957. 31 minutes, color. French narration with English subtitles. Distributed by McGraw-Hill Text Films, 1221 Avenue of the Americas, New York, N. Y. 10020. This is an important documentary film portraying Nazi death camps and the results of the Holocaust. Teachers might begin discussion by asking, "Who was responsible?" Some of the scenes are shocking and gruesome. Some students may be sickened. The teacher is cautioned to preview this film before screening to determine suitability for a particular class. Recommended for mature high school students. It should *not* be shown to junior high or younger groups.

Puppets, a film produced in West Germany, is available from the Anti-Defamation League of B'nai B'rith, 315 Lexington Avenue, New York, N. Y. 10016, 1974. 11 minutes, color. This short film explains totalitarianism through the vehicle of a puppet actor who steps out of his role in a marionette performance of Julius Caesar to serve as backstage guide through history, introducing the audience to infamous charlatans and despots and their victims. He reveals how these villains, including Mussolini, Hitler and Goebbels, used the scapegoat technique to gain the adherence of their followers while duping them out of their freedom. Particularly suitable for junior high school audiences.

Verdict For Tomorrow, a film produced by Capital City Broadcasting Company, 1961. 30 minutes, black and white. Available from the Anti-Defamation League of B'nai B'rith, 315 Lexington Avenue, New York, N. Y. 10016. This film is a well-documented account of the Eichmann trial, and is narrated by Lowell Thomas. The film is based on actual footage gathered during the trial in Jerusalem and utilizes the trial as a reminder of Nazism and Jewish persecution. Recommended for high school audiences.

Warsaw Ghetto, a film produced by BBC-TV, London, England, 1966. 51 minutes, black and white. Distributed by Time-Life Films, Inc., 43 West 16th Street, New York, N. Y. 10011. This is a powerful documentary of Nazi brutality during the Holocaust. It is based largely on German army footage. Some scenes are gruesome and may be upsetting. The teacher is cautioned to preview this film before screening to determine suitability for a particular class. Highly recommended for senior high school groups, but *not* for junior high or younger audiences.

Writings of the Nazi Holocaust, a film produced by the Anti-Defamation League of B'nai B'rith in cooperation with the Archdiocese of New York, 1969. 30 minutes, black and white. Available through the Anti-Defamation League of B'nai B'rith, 315 Lexington Avenue, New York, N. Y. 10016. The Nazi Holocaust is seared into the memory of mankind yet, with the single exception of the *Diary of Anne Frank,* the literature which emerged from these years of madness is virtually unknown. Ernst Pawel, critic and novelist, analyzes the literary merits of what has come to be known as Holocaust literature and interprets its relevance today. Sequences from several works are read by leading actors. A dramatic presentation. Recommended for junior and senior high school audiences.

Jews have been concerned with civil rights and the Black struggle for freedom. Abraham Heschel, (hatless and bearded) a distinguished Jewish religious leader, marched in Selma, Alabama with Martin Luther King, Jr.

CHAPTER VIII

TODAY

Contemporary America

Today, America's Jews are an urban people found in all walks of life and on all economic levels. There are approximately six million Jews in the United States, though the exact number is not known because the Census Bureau is not permitted to ask questions about religion. Jews constitute somewhat less than three percent of all Americans. More than 65% of American Jews live in New York, Chicago, Los Angeles, Philadelphia, Boston, and Miami Beach. Ever increasing numbers of them have left the factories for better jobs in business and the professions. Many are self-employed. In large numbers Jews have become judges, lawyers, doctors, researchers, social scientists, journalists, teachers, musicians, and skilled tradesmen. Most American Jews are middle class, though some are still very poor. In New York City alone recent investigations have revealed at least 250,000 Jews living below the poverty line.

In contemporary America, Jews are more accepted than at any time in the past. Exposure of the horrors of the German and Polish concentration camps at the end of World War II brought an end to most of the vicious, overt anti-Semitism in the United States. Living skeletons emerging from Buchenwald and Auschwitz and Dachau showed the world where anti-Semitism can lead. Hitler's barbaric slaughter of six million Jews shocked Americans into dropping most discrimination against Jews. Prosperity and government legislation also improved the position of Jews and other minority groups. However, both a *Fortune* magazine poll in 1947 and a University of California study in 1969 sponsored by the Anti-Defamation League of B'nai B'rith showed nearly one-third of all Americans still hold hostile feelings toward Jews.

Since World War II, however, discrimination in all areas has significantly diminished. Few colleges have quotas now, and the percentage of young Jewish men and women attending college is greater than their percentage of the population. In public schools and on college campuses Jewish youth have developed a rapport with non-Jews which their grandparents did not experience. Though relatively few in numbers, Jews are usually referred to as one of the three major American religious groups. While many American Jews see themselves as members of an ethnic minority, they also identify with the non-Jewish, middle-class majority, differing only in religion. Most of today's Jews are native-born and the percentage is steadily increasing.

Jewish Education

The synagogue is unquestionably the strongest institution in the Jewish community. Hundreds of new synagogues, Reform, Conservative, and Orthodox, were built as a result of the population shifts following World War II. The process continues as new neighborhoods and new suburbs develop. In some cases Jewish social and recreational centers are the focus of Jewish life, but, lacking the religious component, they offer little serious competition to the synagogues which have frequently incorporated social and educational facilities. Classrooms and community facilities are usually prominent in modern buildings designed by leading architects. Today about sixty percent of American Jews maintain synagogue affiliation, slightly less than the figure for church membership among Christians. In recent decades there has been a remarkable increase in the number of children receiving some form of Jewish education. There has also been a substantial growth in the number of Jewish day schools which parallel the regular grades in public school and combine secular and religious instruction under one roof, eliminating the need for after school or Sunday classes. A large percentage are Orthodox day schools, frequently called "yeshivahs." Several hundred Jewish day schools exist today in the United States.

The synagogue is unquestionably the strongest institution in the Jewish community. Above, the Beth Sholom Synagogue in Elkins Park, Pennsylvania, designed by the distinguished American architect, Frank Lloyd Wright.

A small but growing number of Jewish parents see in the day school a desirable alternative to Sunday schools, capable of producing more knowledgeable and observant children, better able to preserve their Jewish identity. Moreover, second and third generation Jews no longer feel the need of public education in order to validate their American identity, as their immigrant parents and grandparents did.

Jews and Liberalism

Jews have been among the strongest defenders of civil rights and civil liberties in the United States. They read and support liberal publications and have consistently been shown by public opinion polls to hold liberal views. It would be an oversimplification to argue that Jewish religious tradition accounts for these attitudes, although the religion does teach a tradition of social justice. More likely Jews have been influenced by their history. Denied the rights of citizenship in Europe, they adopted liberal or radical positions in order to ameliorate their own condition and have been predominantly committed to the liberal cause ever since. Many American Jews have expanded their own struggle for equality to a struggle for equal treatment for all groups in the United States.

Consequently, Jews have been among the supporters of socially progressive legislation, even after their departure from the sweatshops, and they have been keenly interested in social justice for all of America's minorities, not just for themselves. For example, in 1913 the B'nai B'rith set up an Anti-Defamation League to protect Jews when they faced discrimination. Today the Anti-Defamation League works for the rights of all Americans and combats discrimination against all minority groups.

Similarly American Jews have generally been among the most passionate supporters of the separation of church and state mandated by the First Amendment and of the Supreme Court decisions which have defined such separation. Supreme Court decisions have banned religious observance in public schools and have increasingly emphasized the secular nature of public institutions in America. The Jewish position on matters of church and state was, perhaps, best stated early in the century by a Reform rabbi, Joseph Krauskopf, of Philadelphia, who declared, "Let us be Protestants or Catholics, agnostics or Jews in our churches or homes; in our public institutions, however, let us be Americans."

More recently this issue has shifted from separation of church and state in public schools to government aid to private schools. Until very recently most American Jews strongly opposed federal aid to parochial schools, viewing it as a violation of the principle of separation of church and state. However, some Jewish parents, now dissatisfied with public education, are turning to the Jewish day school, and find themselves on the same side of the issue as parents of Catholic school children in desiring public money for parochial schools.

Jews have been concerned with civil rights and the Blacks. In 1909 when the National Association for the Advancement of Colored People was formed, Rabbi Stephen Wise, founder of New York's Free Synagogue, was among its incorporators. He gave it devoted service for the next forty years. Numerous Jews, among them the prominent attorney Louis Marshall, have served on the board of trustees of the NAACP and have helped in raising funds for the organization. Marshall was also active in other aspects of the civil rights movement, particularly in the struggle against the Ku Klux Klan. Jews have been involved in the movement since shortly after the Civil War, when Julius Rosenwald, the merchandising genius who built Sears, Roebuck and Company, contributed large sums to further Black education.

Following the 1954 Supreme Court desegregation decision, rabbis throughout the South strongly opposed segregation, notwithstanding the pressure of numerous white citizens' groups against them. Jewish religious buildings in Charlotte, Miami, and Nashville were bombed, but rabbis and other Jewish leaders were undaunted in their support for the civil rights movement. A large number of Jews participated in the Freedom Marches of the sixties. The most publicized murder of civil rights workers was that of Michael Schwerner, Andrew Goodman and James E. Chaney. Both Schwerner and Goodman were Jews. Abraham Heschel, a distinguished Jewish religious leader, marched in Selma with Martin Luther King, Jr.

Although a rash of swastikas and hate slogans appeared on the walls of Jewish buildings, stores, and synagogues in 1959 and early 1960, the general trend has been away from expressions of anti-Semitism. Though it is still exploited by extremists at both ends of the political spectrum, anti-Semitism has been so thoroughly discredited by the Nazi excesses that overt expressions of anti-Jewish sentiment within the political mainstream are rare. Nonetheless, Jews remain alert to illiberal movements or any new insensitivity which may threaten them.

Today's Jewish community, generally secure in American society, and possibly the most successful of immigrant groups, perpetuates the traditional Jewish concern for social justice for all. Its attention focuses as much on liberal causes at home as it does on the well-being of the Jewish people elsewhere in the world. In recent years American Jews have been concerned about the State of Israel and the plight of the Jewish community in Russia. But in their own home, American Jews face the future confident of their security in a constitutional democracy which has made America, for them, perhaps more than for any other people, a new world.

TO THE TEACHER:

Chapter 8 opens with a demographic sketch of the contemporary American Jewish community. The movement of substantial numbers of Americans, Jews as well as non-Jews, to suburbia has been an important feature of contemporary life. Inherent in the pattern are a number of social studies themes. The teacher might prompt discussion with such questions as, "What happened to the older Jewish neighborhoods when Jews moved out?" "Who took their places?"

Students should be encouraged to identify and perhaps visit these neighborhoods in their own cities, Jewish as well as other ethnic neighborhoods.

The high regard in which scholarship and learning are held by Jews accounts in part for their educational attainments. As in the preceding chapter, this should be dealt with as a lesson in values. The construction of hundreds of new synagogues after World War II, in part a consequence of the Jewish exodus to suburbia, should be related to questions of identity, self-image, and ethnic survival in America.

The proliferation of Jewish day schools should encourage discussion of public, parochial, and private education. With the growth of the Jewish day school movement, paralleled by an increasing enrollment in private schools, one might ask, "Are public schools again becoming the 'pauper schools' they were in the nineteenth century, reserved for those students whose parents cannot afford private education?"

The remainder of the chapter deals with Jewish concern for social problems in American society, and generates a number of provocative questions. For one thing, what is social justice? Why have Jews traditionally embraced the Democratic party? How does their political behavior contrast with that of other ethnic groups? How does Jewish history influence Jewish political attitudes? Is the traditional support of Jews for the strict separation of church and state weakening as more Jewish parents embrace private education and Jewish day schools? Will Jews now become more hospitable to state aid for parochial schools?

The concern of Jews for the civil rights of Black people and their support for the NAACP and other Black defense organizations could stimulate discussion of Negro-Jewish relations in American history. The problems of Blacks might be fruitfully contrasted to those which Jews have faced in American society. Jews, for example, have generally opposed ethnic quotas in determining employment and admissions policies. They have found that the merit system opens opportunities for them and now feel challenged by a new quota system favoring other minorities. Surely, here is an excellent topic for classroom debate.

DISCUSSION QUESTIONS AND STUDENT ACTIVITIES

1. Before their expulsion from Spain in 1492, Jews enjoyed a Golden Age. Imagine you are a researcher three hundred years from now, studying American civilization. How would you describe American Jewry of today? Is it enjoying another Golden Age? Consider the following:
   - money-raising activities
   - number of books published by and about Jews
   - Jewish education
   - number of Jews in professions and receiving graduate degrees
   - number of Jewish organizations
   - income level
   - role of Jews in American politics
   - Jewish religious activity
   - scientific accomplishments of Jews
   - Jewish artists, writers, and musicians.
2. Ask students to share with the class the kind of religious training they received or are receiving. What features are unique to each denomination? What common features exist among them all?
3. In recent years there has been growing concern in the United States over the question of federal and state aid to parochial schools. Conduct a debate in your class on the following topic: Resolved: Aid to private, religious schools is unconstitutional because it violates the doctrine of separation of church and state as set forth in the First Amendment to the Constitution.
4. Write a comparative review of the books *Jews, Justice and Judaism,* by Robert St. John, and *Justice and Judaism* by Albert Vorspan and Eugene Lipman (listed in the bibliography of this chapter). What emphasis does each place on Jewish values as opposed to Jewish experience, e.g. per-

secution and discrimination, in explaining the Jew's concern for social justice?

5. Consider Rabbi Joseph Krauskopf's statement, "Let us be Protestants or Catholics, agnostics or Jews in our churches or homes; in our public institutions, however, let us be Americans." In light of his comment conduct a discussion on the following topics: 1) Christmas tree and Hanukah menorahs in public schools. (Does the inclusion of one justify the other?) 2) Christmas and Easter programs in public schools. 3) The role of prayers in public schools (relate to recent Supreme Court decisions).
6. Does the study of the Bible as history or literature violate the Supreme Court's ban on Bible reading in the public schools? When should it be, or not be permitted?
7. Prepare a report on the history of the National Association for the Advancement of Colored People. How extensively have Jews been involved in its organization and program? You might begin by looking up biographical material on Rabbi Stephen Wise and Louis Marshall.
8. Read and report on the following publications which discuss the connection between radical political movements and anti-Semitism: Seymour Martin Lipset and Earl Raab, *The Politics of Unreason, Right-Wing Extremism in America, 1790-1970* (Harper Torchbooks, New York, 1973); Benjamin R. Epstein and Arnold Forster, *The New Anti-Semitism* (New York, McGraw-Hill, 1974); and Seymour Martin Lipset, *The Left, The Jews and Israel,* subtitled, *The Socialism of Fools,* published by the Anti-Defamation League of B'nai B'rith (see appendix for address).

BIBLIOGRAPHY

Cohen, Henry, *Justice, Justice: A Jewish View of the Black Revolution* (Union of American Hebrew Congregations, New York, 1969, revised edition, paperback). Summarizes major findings in the social sciences concerning race relations and examines them in light of Jewish theological, historical, and traditional values. The author traces the background of the "Black Revolution," compares Black self-determination and Jewish nationalism, deals with the question of responsibility, and takes a new look at "Black anti-Semitism." This is a thought-provoking book, suitable for teachers and high school students. Discussion questions interspersed throughout the text make it especially useful for teachers in planning lessons.

Forster, Arnold, and Epstein, Benjamin R., *The New Anti-Semitism* (McGraw-Hill, New York, 1974). Available in hard cover and ADL soft cover edition. Based on a study by the Anti-Defamation League of B'nai B'rith. The authors describe the subtle and dangerous forms of anti-Semitism found in the United States today. Recommended for teachers and capable high school students.

Glazer, Nathan, *American Judaism* (University of Chicago, Press, Second Edition, Chicago, 1972, also paperback). Chapter 6 includes material on the sociological characteristics and religious attitudes of the eastern European immigrants, as well as their educational, social, and economic mobility. Chapter 7, "The Jewish Revival" details the renewed religious interests of the children of the eastern European Jewish immigrants as they moved to the suburbs. Recommended for teachers and capable high school students.

Glock, Charles Y., and Stark, Rodney, *Christian Beliefs and Anti-Semitism* (Harper Torchbooks, New York, 1969, paperback). This book is a study of the ways in which the teachings of Christian churches shape American attitudes toward Jews. For teachers and capable high school students.

Goldstein, Sidney, "American Jewry, 1970, A Demographic Profile," in *American Jewish Yearbook* Vol. 72, pp. 3-88, (Jewish Publication Society, Philadelphia, 1971). This is a detailed social-demographic study of the contemporary American Jewish community. Technical and recommended primarily for teachers.

Gordon, Albert I., *Jews in Suburbia* (Beacon Press, Boston, 1959). A sociological survey of contemporary Jewish life in suburban communities. Especially good on the Jewish population shift to the suburbs and the role of the family, synagogue, and ritual in suburbia. Recommended for teachers and high school students.

Marx, Gary, *Protest and Prejudice, a Study of Belief in the Black Community* (Harper & Row, New York, 1967, also in paperback). This work represents part of the Patterns of American Prejudice series conducted by the Survey Research Center of the University of California for the Anti-Defamation League of B'nai B'rith. The first nation-wide study of Black attitudes. Includes material on attitudes toward Jews. Foreword by Bayard Rustin. Suitable for teachers and capable high school students.

Rose, Peter, *The Ghetto and Beyond, Essays on Jewish Life in America* (Random House, New York, 1969). A series of essays dealing with sociological and political aspects of contemporary Judaism. Suitable for teachers and capable high school students.

Selznick, Gertrude J., and Steinberg, Stephen, *The Tenacity of Prejudice* (Harper Torchbooks, New York, 1971, paperback). Subtitled, *Anti-Semitism in Contemporary America*, this is the first intensive study of prejudice using survey data based on a nation-wide sample of Americans. The study concludes that the better educated the person, the less likely he is to hold prejudiced beliefs. For teachers and capable high school students.

Sherman, C. Bezalel, *The Jews Within American Society: A Study in Ethnic Individuality* (Wayne State University Press, Detroit, 1961, also in paperback). An important study which shows that Jews in America, unlike other European immigrant groups, have withstood the forces of assimilation and remained the only white ethnic group to retain all the characteristic features of a minority. Recommended primarily for teachers and capable high school students.

Sklare, Marshall, *America's Jews* (Random House, New York, 1971, paperback). An important sociological study of the contemporary Jewish community in America. The foreword by Peter Rose is excellent. His criteria for ethnic studies are a "must" for teachers. Professor Sklare provides a wealth of material on social characteristics of American Jews. Special areas include the Jewish community, Jewish education, and intermarriage. Recommended for teachers and capable high school students.

Sklare, Marshall, (editor), *The Jews: Social Patterns of an American Group* (The Free Press, New York, 1958). In this work Professor Sklare pulls together a number of important studies made during the forties and fifties. Section 2 contains excellent demographic studies. Section 3 deals with social and structural patterns in the Jewish community. Section 5 relates to questions of Jewish identity. Recommended for teachers and advanced students doing research.

St. John, Robert, *Jews, Justice and Judaism* (Doubleday, New York, 1969). Chapters 23 through 28 deal with a number of topics in this chapter. St. John's main thrust throughout the book is the involvement of Jews with justice, which he tends to see as a function of Jewish values and concepts. However, he minimizes the influence of persecution and anti-Semitism which until fairly recently denied equality to Jews and more than likely account for many Jewish attitudes. Recommended for teachers and high school students.

Vorspan, Albert, *Giants of Justice* (Crowell, New York, 1960). Contains profiles of fourteen outstanding Jews who have influenced the course of American democracy. Written in a straightforward style which makes it suitable for junior and senior high school students.

Vorspan, Albert and Lipman, Eugene J., *Justice and Judaism* (Union of American Hebrew Congregations, New York, 1956). An attempt to relate Jewish attitudes and thought to the concept of justice in contemporary America. Deals with a number of areas of social concern, such as housing, education, civil rights and liberties, religious liberty, interreligious activity, immigration, and others. Written primarily for Jews, but will be very useful for all faiths. Recommended for teachers and high school students.

Weyl, Nathaniel, *The Jew In American Politics* (Arlington House, New Rochelle, N. Y., 1968). Chapters 1 through 13 of this excellent book give an overview of American Jewish history, with emphasis on its political aspects. Chapters 14 through 20 present a social-political analysis of contemporary Jewish society. The book is especially good on civil rights, Zionism, and church-state matters. Recommended primarily for teachers and advanced high school students.

AUDIO-VISUAL MATERIALS

The American Jewish Writer, an illustrated film-lecture, produced by the Anti-Defamation League of B'nai B'rith in cooperation with the Archdiocese of New York, 1969. 30 minutes, black and white. Available from the Anti-Defamation League of B'nai B'rith, 315 Lexington Avenue, New York, N. Y. 10016. Discusses the emergence during the last 25 years of a number of Jewish authors who, unlike their predecessors who wrote solely for a Jewish audience, now address themselves to Christians and non-Christians alike. Louis Zara, critic, editor and novelist, examines the twentieth century American-Jewish experience and the reason for its universal appeal. Mr. Zara draws on the works of Bernard Malamud, Saul Bellow and Philip Roth. Excerpts from their writings are read by Norman Rose, TV and film actor. Recommended for high school audiences.

Call For the Question: The Synagogue in the Community, a filmstrip produced by Samuel Grand, 1957. 53 frames, color, with recorded narration and 2 copies of teacher's manual. Distributed by the Union of American Hebrew

Congregations, 838 Fifth Ave., New York, N. Y. 10021. This production portrays the role of the synagogue in social action and the impact of civil rights, housing, juvenile delinquency, and segregation on the synagogue in America. It is a thought-provoking filmstrip which relates some of the social problems confronting the nation to Jewish ethical concepts. Suitable for high school students.

Israel: A Story of the Jewish People, a film produced by the International Film Foundation, 1967. 30 minutes, color. Distributed by the Anti-Defamation League of B'nai B'rith, 315 Lexington Avenue, New York, N. Y. 10016. In telling the 4,000-year history of the Jewish people, this film traces their dramatic journey from the Fertile Crescent through the Diaspora and back to the young State of Israel. Animation sequences illustrate the earliest periods and focus on individuals who stress the unity of the Jewish people with their land. Still photographs document the early pioneering days in Palestine, the horrors of the Holocaust, the creation of the modern State of Israel and the return of European refugees to their spiritual homeland. Film footages are used to portray Israel today, her social and economic problems and her achievements which have been made in a climate of continued conflict with her Arab neighbors. Recommended for junior and senior high school audiences.

Major Noah, a filmstrip produced and distributed by the Jewish Education Committee of New York, 426 W. 58th St., New York, N. Y. 10019, 1967. 40 frames, color. Includes two copies of accompanying script. This is an entertaining and informative filmstrip about Mordecai Manuel Noah, who served as U.S. consul in the early 19th century and also attempted to settle the world's Jews on an island in the Niagara River preparatory to their ultimate relocation in Palestine. Historically, the story of Noah's life belongs in an earlier chapter, but his proto-Zionist activities warrant his inclusion in here. Recommended for junior and senior high school audiences.

Rabbi Stephen S. Wise: A Twentieth Century Prophet, a filmstrip produced by Samuel Grand, 1956. 43 frames, black and white. Includes 2 copies of teacher's guide. A 12-inch LP recorded narration is available, (containing excerpts spoken by Rabbi Wise). Sponsored and distributed by the Commission on Jewish Education, Union of American Hebrew Congregations, 838 Fifth Ave., New York, N. Y. 10021. This filmstrip portrays the life of Rabbi Wise, a leader in the Zionist and cultural affairs of the American Jewish community. It is informative, accurate, and interesting. The artwork is good. Suitable for high school audiences.

Sometime Before Morning, a documentary film produced and distributed by the Anti-Defamation League of B'nai B'rith, 315 Lexington Avenue, New York, N. Y. 10016, 1973. 30 minutes, color. In honor of its sixtieth anniversary the Anti-Defamation League produced this film about its work in education, in promoting better intergroup relations, and in protecting minority groups. This film, however, is much more than that, since it shows the state of prejudice in the nation and dramatically portrays the role of the ADL in helping achieve justice and equality for all. Recommended for high school audiences.

The Work of My Hands, a film produced by Allen d'Or Productions, Inc., 1959. 15 minutes, color. Sponsored and distributed by the Commission on Social Action of Reform Judaism, Union of American Hebrew Congregations, 838 Fifth Ave., New York, N. Y. 10021. This film was prepared as an aid in encouraging social action among Jews. It relates Jewish ethical values to urgent social issues, such as race relations and civil liberties. Recommended for high school audiences.

APPENDIX

Sources of Additional Resource Materials

AMERICAN ASSOCIATION FOR JEWISH EDUCATION
114 Fifth Ave.
New York, N. Y. 10011

AMERICAN JEWISH COMMITTEE
165 East 56th Street
New York, New York 10022

AMERICAN JEWISH CONGRESS
15 East 84th Street
New York, New York 10028

ANTI-DEFAMATION LEAGUE OF B'NAI B'RITH
315 Lexington Avenue
New York, New York 10016

NATIONAL ACADEMY FOR ADULT JEWISH STUDIES
218 East 70th Street
New York, New York 10021

NATIONAL CONFERENCE OF CHRISTIANS AND JEWS
43 West 57th Street
New York, New York 10019

NATIONAL JEWISH WELFARE BOARD
15 East 26th Street
New York, New York 10010

JEWISH AGENCY
Department of Education & Culture
515 Park Avenue
New York, New York 10022

JEWISH NATIONAL FUND
Department of Education & Youth
42 East 69th Street
New York, New York 10021

INDEX

Authors and Titles

Names